The Vinyl Dialogues Volume IV

"From Studio to Stylus"

Mike Morsch

Cover photo by Mat Shetler, taken at Morningstar Studios in East Norriton, Pennsylvania, courtesy of Glenn Barratt

Cover design by Mat Shetler and David Munoz-Mendoza

Editing by Frank Quattrone, Aubrey Huston, and Gemini Wordsmiths: Ruth Littner and Ann Stolinsky

ISBN: 978-1-62249-408-8

Published by Biblio Publishing
BiblioPublishing.com

Table of Contents

Introduction

There is a scene in the Broadway show *Beautiful: The Carole King Musical* where King is offering the song "Will You (Still) Love Me Tomorrow" to the all-girl group the Shirelles.

Written by King and then-husband and songwriting partner Gerry Goffin, the Shirelles' lead singer Shirley Olson (later Shirley Alston Reeves) at first didn't like the song. She thought it was "too country" and didn't want the group to record it.

But the Shirelles did eventually record the song and it would become the first song by an all-girl African-American group to reach No. 1 on the charts in the United States after its release in 1960. And it would be the first No. 1 hit that Goffin and King would write.

The scene helps advance the storyline of the hit musical, which is still appearing on Broadway as of 2017.

While *Beautiful: The Carole King Musical* details King's recollections and perspective on her career from its beginning up through the time of the making of her first solo album *Tapestry* in 1971, Shirley Alston Reeves' account of that story — of King pitching "Will You (Still) Love Me Tomorrow" to the Shirelles — is included in this volume of *The Vinyl Dialogues*. And it helps illustrate what this series has been about since its inception: Not many artists will be fortunate enough to have a Broadway musical written about their careers, shows that detail the inspirations for the songs and the stories behind the making of their albums.

The Vinyl Dialogues does record and preserve those stories from the perspectives of the artists who made up the soundtracks of our lives.

Up to this point, the series has been about albums made in the 1970s, which happens to be my decade, the period when I was in both high school and college.

In *Volume IV: From Studio to Stylus,* I decided to include details of some albums made in the 1960s. People have asked me why I haven't advanced the series to include albums from the 1980s. The answer is that by the time the 1980s rolled around, I was focused on career, marriage and fatherhood. I just didn't connect with much with the music from that decade.

But the 1960s music — the records that my parents had in their vinyl collection — provided the foundation for my musical tastes. Since there are a lot of happy memories for me associated with that music, I wanted to explore some albums from that decade.

And that decision has not been a disappointment. While there are still many albums from the 1970s detailed in this volume, I was thrilled to be able to talk to some highly accomplished artists of the 1960s. In addition to Shirley Alston Reeves, I had wonderful conversations with Marilyn McCoo and Billy Davis Jr. of the 5th Dimension; Peter Noone of Herman's Hermits; Felix Cavaliere of the Rascals; Peter Yarrow of Peter, Paul and Mary; and Bob Berryhill of the Surfaris, among others.

It's made for a diverse and eclectic group of well-known — and some not-so-well-known — albums from the 1960s and 1970s that are detailed in this volume.

The music from these two decades has stood the test of time. And it never gets old.

So sit back and drop the needle on this next group of albums.

— Mike Morsch

A good night to write a hit song

Tonight's the Night
The Shirelles
(1961)

The Shirelles had two singles that charted in the late 1950s — "I Met Him on a Sunday" in 1958, and "Dedicated to the One I Love" in 1959 — but neither had broken into the Top 40.

One of the first all-girl groups of that era, the Shirelles — Shirley Owens (later Shirley Alston Reeves), Doris Coley (later Doris Kenner-Jackson), Addie "Micki" Harris (later Addie Harris McFadden), and Beverly Lee — were signed in the early 1960s by Florence Greenberg for the newly formed Scepter Records.

"The record company didn't ask us; it told us to do an album," said Shirley Alston Reeves. "We were about to record in the studio and Florence Greenberg, who owned the label, said, 'Why don't you girls write another song?' We had written 'I Met Him on a Sunday,' our first record. And Florence said, 'You can make money writing, so go home and write a song.' I said, 'When do you want us to do it?' And she said, 'Tonight.' I said, 'OK, tonight's the night.' And I went home and I wrote it. It was as simple as that."

The song is about a woman who is both hesitant and expectant over her first sexual experience, an edgy proposition to sing about in a song in the early 1960s. The lyrics included the words "You said you're gonna meet me, tonight's the night. You said you're gonna kiss me, tonight's

Shirley Alston Reeves, along with Luther Dixon, co-wrote and sang lead on the title track "Tonight's the Night," which got to No. 39 on the U.S. Billboard Top 100 Singles chart. (Photo by Mike Morsch)

the night. … I might love you so. … Turn the lights down low, you said you're gonna make me feel all aglow. Well, I don't know, well I don't know right now, I might love you so."

"The other girls really liked it. We just sat down and got it together and sang it and it came out real good," said Alston Reeves.

Upon hearing the song, Greenberg paired Owens with Luther Dixon, who had already worked with Perry Como, Nat King Cole, and Pat Boone. Dixon would add to the song, eventually sharing songwriting credit with Owens, and produce the single.

The song was released in September 1960 and went gold in 1961. That success prompted Scepter Records officials to urge the Shirelles to record an album.

Carole King, who along with husband Gerry Goffin wrote "Will You (Still) Love Me Tomorrow," pitched the song to the Shirelles and it went all the way to No. 1 on the Billboard Hot 100 singles chart and became a million-seller for the group.
(Photo by Phil McAuliffe)

"Tonight's the Night" would become the title track to the Shirelles' debut album of the same name, also released in 1961. It would become the first single from the album, and it cracked the Top 40, coming in at No. 39 on the U.S. Billboard Top 100 Singles chart.

But the follow-up single from that album really put the Shirelles on the map. Written by Carole King and Gerry Goffin, "Will You (Still) Love Me Tomorrow" went all the way to No. 1 on the Billboard Hot 100 chart and became a million-seller.

King and Goffin had met in college in the late 1950s and began a songwriting collaboration — with King writing the music and Goffin writing the lyrics — as well as a personal relationship. When King became pregnant in August 1959, they married. Goffin was 20 years old and King was 17.

Both secured jobs at Aldon Music, a New York-based music publishing company founded by Al Nevins and Don Kirshner and in 1958. Aldon would end up playing a significant role in the development of what was called the Brill Building Sound in the late 1950s and 1960s.

The Brill Building, an office building at 1619 Broadway on 49th Street in Manhattan, housed scores of music publishers and songwriting teams, including Burt Bacharach and Hal David, Tommy Boyce and Bobby Hart, Neil Sedaka and Howard Greenfield, Jerry Leiber and Mike Stoller, Barry Mann and Cynthia Weil; and solo songwriters including Sonny Bono, Neil Diamond, Marvin Hamlisch, Laura Nyro, Paul Simon, Phil Spector, and Steve Tyrell.

It was that creative environment that Goffin and King entered.

But when King first pitched "Will You (Still) Love Me" to the Shirelles, Alston Reeves didn't like it at all.

"Carole came in and she played it on the piano and sang it for us. And I looked at Florence, I said, 'Let me tell you, that's not a Shirelles record.' She said, 'What do you mean?'

I said, 'I'm telling you, that's a Country Western song and we don't do Country Western. I don't think it's gonna work,'" said Alston Reeves.

"It was the way Carole was singing and how she was playing it. There were no strings or anything. She was just banging it out on the piano and singing it," said Alston Reeves. "And she sang with a little drawl. It wasn't a Southern thing, but the song was slow."

Greenberg didn't hear it the same way, though, and wanted the Shirelles to cut the song anyway.

"Florence said, 'If it doesn't work, we'll just put it on the album; maybe it will come out better.' That's what they used to do then; they would stick things on the album that they didn't think were going to be hits for filler," said Alston Reeves. "A lot of times, though, that's when a good one comes out. It does happen at times."

Alston Reeves changed her mind, though, when it came time to record the song.

"When I got to the studio with the girls and we got the music team and started with the strings and everything, we fell in love with the song. It was beautiful," said Alston Reeves. "After that, whenever we had to record, Florence would ask me what I thought was not a good Shirelles song, and that's what we'd put out. Florence would say, 'Let's ask Shirley what she thinks isn't going to make it.'"

Another song on the *Tonight's the Night* album that got some attention — but not until a few years later when it was recorded by another group — was "Boys," written by Dixon and Wes Farrell. It was the B-side of "Will You (Still) Love Me Tomorrow."

The other band that covered it? The Beatles.

The song, recorded in one take at Abbey Road Studios on February 11, 1963, was included on the Beatles' first album released in the United Kingdom, *Please Please Me* in

1963. It's also notable because the song is the first recorded lead vocal by Beatles drummer Ringo Starr.

In a 2005 interview with *Rolling Stone*, Paul McCartney said "Boys" was a favorite of Beatles fans in the band's early years in the UK.

"It was great, though, if you think about It — here's us doing a song and it was a girl's song. 'I talk about the boys now!' Or it was a gay song. But we never even listened," McCartney said in the *Rolling Stone* interview. "It's just a great song. I think that's one of the things about youth — you just don't give a shit. I love the innocence of those days."

The Shirelles liked the Beatles' version of "Boys."

"It's just a little old rock and roll song. No heavy lyrics, but there are a lot of hits that didn't have many lyrics. The Beatles' version was a combination of singer and song," said Alston Reeves. "I hate to say it, but we didn't know then who the Beatles were the first time we were asked about them. We had to pretend we knew who they were. Then after we heard their version, we said we have to find out who the Beatles are. But we loved their version right away. Their sound was different and very tight."

The album cover for *Tonight's the Night* doesn't show the Shirelles. Instead, the cover shows a lacy pink dress on the floor next to a small table covered by a gold cloth. A letter on the table sits alongside a photo of an unrecognizable white male. On the floor next to the table and dress is a bouquet of roses with a card that reads, "Dedicated to the One I Love," which is the name of the first track on Side Two of the album.

"Florence had gone to the store, a five-and-dime somewhere, and bought a little round table and a picture frame. It had a picture of some guy, a model, I don't know, a handsome guy," said Alston Reeves. "We said, 'Why can't we have our picture on the cover, like some of the other artists?' But the record company officials said it was because a lot of the white people would not want their children to have albums sitting in their homes with black artists on it. So we said, OK."

"Dedicated to the One I Love," written by Lowman Pauling and Ralph Bass, was originally a hit for the "5" Royales in 1957. The Shirelles first covered the song in 1959 and it reached No. 83 on the Billboard Hot 100 Singles chart. The group re-released it as a single in 1961, and it climbed to No. 3 on the Billboard Hot 100

Singles chart and No. 2 on the Billboard R&B chart, and was subsequently included on the *Tonight's the Night* album.

Despite the hit singles, the *Tonight's the Night* album failed to chart on the U.S. Billboard 200 Albums chart. But more positively, the Shirelles and the *Tonight's the Night* album have been credited with launching the girl group genre, that included music accepted by both black and white audiences. This laid the groundwork for success by later girl groups from Motown, like the Supremes.

Two of the songs from the Shirelles' debut album — "Tonight's the Night" and "Will You (Still) Love Me Tomorrow" — were selected by *Rolling Stone* to be on its list of the greatest songs of all time.

"In that field, we were one of the first girl groups. I think we opened the doors. But it didn't even brush past us that we were setting any kind of trend. We were just doing it and having fun," said Alston Reeves. "The whole ride was very good. We opened a lot of doors and broke through a lot of barriers. We played in the South when it wasn't favorable to us with segregation. We played the first integrated show in Alabama.

"I think that we made a difference. I can tell you this — we had the right music at the time and people loved our music. That's how we got away with things. And I think we got away with it because we were women, too. I don't know if people were intimidated by the guy groups. Most of the places we played we had great audiences and they treated us with respect. There was no funny business," she said.

"I can look back on those days and know that we made a difference. Once people got to see us and learn who we were, not what color we were, but who we were, we got that respect. And the music was just that good."

Discography

The Shirelles
"Tonight's the Night"
Released March 16, 1961

Side one

1 "Tonight's the Night" (Luther Dixon, Shirley Owens)
2 "Johnny on My Mind" (Edward Lyons)
3 "Lower the Flame" (Barney Williams, Eddie Snyder, Stanley Kahan)
4 "Will You Love Me Tomorrow" (Carole King, Gerry Goffin)
5 "Doin' the Ronde" (Addie Harris, Beverly Lee, Doris Coley, Shirley Owens)
6 "You Don't Want My Love" (Luther Dixon)

Side two

1 "Dedicated to the One I Love" (Lowman Pauling, Ralph Bass)
2 "Boys" (Luther Dixon, Wes Farrell)
3 "The Dance Is Over" (Luther Dixon)
4 "Oh, What a Waste of Love" (Allyson R. Khent, Luther Dixon)
5 "Unlucky" (Bobby Banks, Lillian Shockley)
6 "Tonight at the Prom" (Barney Williams, Eddie Snyder, Stanley Kahan)

A broken piece of plywood and a control room yelp

WIPE OUT
The Surfaris
(1963)

One Saturday, Bob Berryhill got a call from his friends Pat Connolly and Jim Fuller. They asked if they could come over to his house in Glendora, California, to practice.

They were all teenage musicians enamored with surf music, and Berryhill had a place in his parents' house set up with guitars and amps. Kids would regularly come over to the Berryhill household and jam, so it wasn't an unusual request.

Berryhill said sure, come on over. It was September 1962, and that day would be the start of a series of events that would lead to the recording of what would become one of the most iconic songs in the history of surf music.

Connolly, Fuller, and Berryhill rehearsed for about three hours that day. Berryhill played all the Ventures' songs that he knew and Fuller played all the Dick Dale songs that he knew. Both of those bands had already made their marks in the world of surf music, the sound that had gripped southern California at the time and were highly regarded by the boys.

"And then Pat said, 'I've got a gig at Pomona Catholic High School tonight. Would you like to play?'" Berryhill recalled Connolly asking. "And I said, 'Well sure, but we don't have a drummer.' A surf band without a drummer, what are you going to do? And Pat said, 'We're going to meet the drummer there.' And if you've ever done music, you just don't show up and play a gig because you have to hope that it's gonna work out."

But it did work out. The drummer was an extremely gifted and talented youngster named Ron Wilson.

"I've always kind of compared Ronnie to John Bonham [drummer for Led Zeppelin] and Keith Moon [drummer for The Who]," said Berryhill. "Ron was kind of a forerunner of that kind of playing, where it was just all over the place. Ronnie would just stand up and on his drums and beat the heck out of them, and then run around the front and click on them. He would just go nuts."

The band played that night at a dance after the high school football game, and the kids at Pomona Catholic High School responded positively.

"Everybody loved what we sounded like as a surf band. We didn't have a microphone and we just played instrumentals through one amplifier and the drums. In the gym, it sounded great to everybody, and that kind of got us going. That was our first opportunity to play," said Berryhill.

The new group still didn't have a name but they continued to practice. Eventually they enlisted the help of Dale Smallin, a local businessman and videographer they all knew, who produced bicycle safety videos. Smallin, they thought, could help get them some more local gigs.

Smallin had a studio in Azusa, California, where the teens would rehearse from time to time. It was at one of those rehearsals one evening that Wilson showed up with a sign painted on his bass drum head that read "The Surfaris." The group had decided to call itself "The Surfaris," as in, surfing safari.

"Dale said, 'Hey, I have to sell you guys; what are you calling yourselves?' We thought were we being real clever calling ourselves 'The Surfaris.' At fifteen years old, you think you're pretty clever and can conquer the world," said Berryhill.

It wouldn't be the last time that creativity would benefit the band as it moved along on the wave of events that would lead them to stardom.

Just a few months later, in November 1962, Wilson again showed up at rehearsal with another idea. He shared with the others that he had a dream about a song called "Surfer Joe."

"Ronnie was a big fan of the Beach Boys and he was a vocalist, so he wanted to sing. The Beach Boys, at that time, were still under the control of their dad, Murry Wilson, and they had 'Surfin' and a few other songs that were being played on the radio," said Berryhill. "So Ron was singing 'Surfer Joe' for me and I started putting a chord progression to it. That was kind of my thing, arranging songs.

"Ronnie basically had a few verses and the chorus. And we had to sit down and write the rest of the verses," said Berryhill. "The famous thing was that there were originally five verses to 'Surfer Joe.' Ronnie had the first three, and we helped him write the next two, a group-think to finish the song out. I did the arrangement of the guitar and music part of it, and Ronnie sang the melody. He's the basic songwriter on 'Surfer Joe' because it's his original stuff."

When Smallin heard the song, he said, "You know, that's a pretty good song. Why don't we record it? I'll find a place," Berryhill recalled.

Smallin enlisted the help of Paul C. Buff, who would go on to be considered the father of surf music recording in California. An ex-Marine who had learned a lot about electronics in his early 20s, Buff had a studio in Cucamonga, California.

"Paul was an innovator of all types. He was kind of like an inventor. He had never built a studio before, but he knew what would come out of it. He was our George Martin," said Berryhill, referring to the legendary Beatles producer.

Some of the other young musicians at the time had recorded at Buff's studio, including Frank Zappa and the Strawberry Alarm Clock.

Smallin eventually secured time at Buff's studio to record "Surfer Joe," but there was still the issue of where the money would come from to do the session.

"We all stood in the driveway of my dad's house on 740 South Grand Avenue in Glendora, California — Dale Smallin, the four of us, my uncle, Don Fisher, just sort of standing there. It was where the rubber meets the road, when the manager says, 'OK, where is the money?' Pat and Jim and Ronnie unfolded their pockets and nothing came out. They all stood there, and Dale was looking at me saying, 'Well, we're not going if we don't have the money,'" recalled Berryhill.

Berryhill went into the house to ask his mother, Katherine, if she would write the check for $150 for the recording session. And she did, for which Berryhill would eventually reimburse her from his band earnings.

"People didn't even make $150 a week in those days. That was almost a month's salary. She just gave me a funny look and said OK," said Berryhill.

This was around early December 1962. The exact date of the recording session has been lost to history, but it was before Christmas, according to Berryhill.

So the band members all piled into two vehicles – Berryhill's truck and Uncle Don Fisher's 1953 Chevy station wagon – and headed for Buff's studio with the check in hand.

The boys did a couple of takes on "Surfer Joe." They had set up one microphone in the middle of the studio and recorded the music part of the song, then went back and overdubbed the vocals, with Wilson singing the lead on all five verses of the song.

When they were finished, everyone seemed satisfied with the recording. Smallin and Buff, who were watching from behind the glass in the recording room, hit the talkback button.

"Boys, you need a second song for your forty-five."

"We go, well, we didn't write another song. At fifteen you're really not prepared for life. We didn't anticipate that situation," said Berryhill.

Buff suggested that if the boys wanted, he could put "Surfer Joe" on both sides of the 45. "Some groups did that," he said.

"We said, no, we'll write another song," said Berryhill.

Wilson got back on the drums and did what he did best and started playing a beat.

"And I thought, well, we'd better put some chords to this with a melody and a baseline or it's going to be a drum solo. Ronnie was that kind of a guy. He'd just take over and start playing," said Berryhill. "And it sounded great."

They recorded it once, and then again and again. After the third take, they had what they wanted. The entire recording session for both songs took about four hours.

"That's what we had in the band; each one of us improvised in our own space. But it worked with Ronnie holding it all together with the drums. It worked due to our special chemistry as a band that held us together while creating the music. It was a culmination of what we knew because we were used to playing four-hour dances," said Berryhill.

When the recording was complete, the question became what to name the song. The week before, Fuller had made a trip to Tijuana, Mexico, where he bought a switchblade, which was illegal to own at the time. He pulled the switchblade out of his pocket, stepped up, and clicked it open over the microphone.

"Let's call it 'Switchblade,'" said Fuller.

But Buff didn't like that. So Berryhill's father, Robert, went outside into the alley behind the studio and found an old cement-soaked piece of plywood and brought it back inside and gave it to Connolly.

"Pat broke it over the microphone and it sounded like a busted surfboard," said Berryhill. "But guess what, there was already a song called 'Bustin' Surfboards.'"

Someone asked, "What causes a busted surfboard?"

A wipeout.

Smallin heard that and came out of the control room and yelled "Ha-ha-ha-ha wipeout!"

"He just yelled it out of nowhere. Nobody had ever heard it before in our lives. So we cracked the board again, Dale yelled out the laugh and we put it on the front of the tape. And two weeks later, we had a forty-five."

"Wipe Out" would be released on the flip side of the "Surfer Joe" 45 record. And nobody could anticipate what was about to happen with the song, and how it would propel The Surfaris into surf music history.

"It was a case, though, where 'Wipe Out' was an instrumental and we were an instrumental band who happened to do a few vocals. 'Wipe Out' really should have been the A-side but 'Surfer Joe' was the reason we had the $150 and why we went out there to the studio," said Berryhill.

It was at this point when the continued series of events and the evolution of "Wipe Out" went into surf music folklore, according to Berryhill.

Once the 45 was pressed — it was labeled as being on DSF (Dale Francis Smallin) Records — Smallin met the boys once again at Berryhill's house, where he brought along 100 copies of the 45 record. He gave each of the band members 25 copies of the record and asked what they wanted to do with them.

"Since we were a group, even though my family and I had paid for the session, it became an 'all-for-one-and-one-for-all' situation, so the records were given out equally," said Berryhill.

According to Berryhill, Fuller planned to take his 25 to school and sell them to his friends so that he could raise money to buy a Stratocaster guitar. Connolly planned to do much the same, because he wanted to make enough money to buy a Fender Precision Bass guitar.

Berryhill had other ideas.

"I said, 'Hold it guys. We want this on the radio so we can buy multiple guitars,'" said Berryhill.

At this point, there had been no contracts signed by the band members, and that would become problematic because all of them were still minors.

The band members decided to let Smallin take the record and try to get it radio play. Unbeknownst to the boys and their parents, Buff had already taken the record to some of the major labels, including Capitol. All passed on it.

Buff had also shopped the record to Art Laboe, a radio disc jockey at KRLA in Los Angeles, but didn't want it, either.

Smallin eventually gave the record to a sales rep at Merritt Distributing Company, where it caught the attention of one of the company's employees, Richard Delvy, who also happened to be the drummer for a group called The Challengers. Delvy in turn gave it to a friend of his, John Marascalco, a songwriter who had written for Little Richard.

Delvy and Marascalco wanted to buy the record for $200. But The Surfaris didn't bite. Behind the boys' backs, the two had already released it on Marascalco's Princess Record label, had edited "Surfer Joe" down to three verses from the original five verses and cut off the ending to "Wipe

Out," ostensibly so that it would be more attractive to AM radio disc jockeys.

Princess Records took the edited songs to KYNO in Fresno, California, and got a disc jockey there to put it into his regular rotation of songs. The company did the same thing with a radio station in San Bernardino, California.

Almost immediately, the record was the most requested song on both stations. Life was about to change for The Surfaris and with it came a boatload of headaches.

Things were moving quickly, but there was still no contract.

On March 21, 1963, Delvy and Marascalco gathered the band members at Berryhill's home. Neither had heard the band play live yet.

"All they knew was that they came to the house and here were three sixteen-year-olds and a seventeen-year-old sitting around a room at my mom and dad's house. They were looking at country bumpkins who didn't know anything. They go, wow, here's a cherry, we can pick this," said Berryhill. "So they had us sign contracts. They already had them printed out. Of course, we couldn't sign contracts because we were under age. But we signed anyway because we were young and inexperienced. They said hey, we've got this going and we're going to give you $1,200. They already offered us money. We said OK."

Delvy and Marascalco then shopped the Princess record to Randy Wood, president of Dot Records. He loved it and agreed to distribute it on the Dot label.

As was oftentimes the case, the disc jockeys flipped over the record, and it was "Wipe Out," not "Surfer Joe," that was the hit. By April 1963, the song had become No. 1 in the Los Angeles market and was starting to make its way around the world. By September 1963, it had reached No. 2 on the Billboard Top 100 Singles chart and was in the Top 10 in Germany, Japan, and Australia.

Once "Wipe Out" began to hit, the phone started ringing. The Surfaris were getting regular gigs at teen dances around southern California. Due to the band's popularity, it had outgrown its regional appeal, and offers began coming in from a wide range of places.

Dot Records decided that it wanted an album to go with the single. So the band once again went to Buff's studio in Cucamonga to record songs to create an album around "Wipe Out" and "Surfer Joe."

"Smallin said, 'Here's a list of songs we want you to record,'" recalled Berryhill. "We said, 'Well, those are on our playlist, but we don't necessarily want to record those songs.' And he said, 'I'm sorry, that's what Dot wants.'"

"So as sixteen-year-old kids, you just do what you're told. We went out on a Saturday and recorded all the songs that Dot wanted except 'Wipe Out' and 'Surfer Joe' for the album," said Berryhill. "What happened was we recorded the list of songs on the album in eight hours in one day. Two weeks later, the album came out. Now in 1963, there was no way we could record an album, get the photography, printing and pressing done in two weeks. You can do a forty-five, but you can't do a whole album. It just didn't happen like that. It took three months to do an album. So we were a little suspicious."

The band's suspicions were well-founded when it came to the *Wipe Out* album.

When the album came out, it had a picture of the five Surfaris on the back, including sax player Jim Pash, who was in the band but had not been at the original recording session for "Surfer Joe" or "Wipe Out."

"He was not there the night we recorded 'Wipe Out' because his mom and dad wanted him to go to Juilliard and they didn't want him infected by young hoodlums playing surf music. They made him stay home because he was only thirteen-years-old at the time," said Berryhill.

Once again, the Berryhill household, where the band had all its meetings, was the scene of the next big moment for The Surfaris, playing the *Wipe Out* album for the band members to hear for the first time.

"The number one song on the A-side is 'Wipe Out,' two minutes, twelve seconds, written by The Surfaris. That plays, and we go wow, that's cool. And then the number two song comes up, 'Wibble Wobble.' And Jim Pash goes, 'That's not me playing the sax,'" recalled Berryhill. "Then the next song comes up, 'Torque.' And Jim says, 'That's not me, either.' And then the next song, 'You Can't Sit Down.' 'That's not me either.' And then we get to 'Green Onions' and that's not my guitar playing. And Ron Wilson goes, 'That's not my drumming either,' on 'Tequila.' And then 'Wild Weekend.' 'Not my sax playing,' Jim said."

Smallin was standing in the room observing the reactions of the band members as they played the album.

"We were having a conniption," said Berryhill. "We asked Dale, 'What happened?'

"He said, 'Well, they overdubbed you a little bit because you're not union musicians.' What a lame excuse," said Berryhill.

The *Wipe Out* album by The Surfaris ended up having only two songs recorded by the band, and no songs that featured saxophonist Jim Pash.

The whole thing ended up in a long, drawn-out court battle, the result of which is that there are five different covers of the *Wipe Out* album — a different one was printed every time a court decision came down in the case.

Pash's family sued Dot Records to have his picture removed from the *Wipe Out* album cover, which resulted in Pash personally receiving several thousands of dollars, and which marked the demise of The Surfaris' contract with Dot Records.

"Dot did not pick up our option to record any further albums, and it was over," said Berryhill.

Despite the legal battles, The Surfaris continued to enjoy popularity. In January 1964, the William Morris Agency had been signed on to represent the band, and the agency secured a spot for them on a 31-date tour of Australia that included the Beach Boys, Roy Orbison, Paul and Paula, and an Australian band called The Joy Boys. Since they were still minors, The Surfaris were accompanied by a chaperone, Jim Pash's brother-in-law.

"Roy Orbison was already an established star. He was idolized in Australia. The British Empire has a whole different feel for music than the United States does. It was like you could hear a pin drop in the auditorium when he was singing. Everybody wanted to hear every word that he said and every note that he sang," said Berryhill. "And the Beach Boys were still being managed by Murry Wilson, who we called 'The Barging Rhino.' He was just a wild man, always cracking the whip on his boys."

At one point during that tour, the bands had a night off, and The Surfaris and the Beach Boys decided to take in a movie.

"At the end of the movie, they played a one-minute video clip of the Beatles. We didn't know who they were. But because Australia was a British colony, they had stuff that we didn't ever see," said Berryhill. "So they played the clip, the house lights came up, and Brian Wilson said, 'They'll never make it.'"

Just a few weeks later, on February 9, 1964, the Beatles appeared on *The Ed Sullivan Show* and the music industry in the United States shifted overnight.

"*The Ed Sullivan Show*, it was over for surf music that night," said Berryhill. "What happened was that after that appearance and people saw their haircuts, that was like a total revelation. Long hair. It was short, but compared to crew cuts, it was long.

"We got back to the U.S. and played a concert up in Sacramento where we had an opening act of guys who were lip-syncing Beatles songs and wearing Beatles wigs. And the crowd was going nuts," said Berryhill. "It was like what a tribute band would be today. They didn't even play, but they were holding their guitars. They just played a tape of the original Beatles album. People bought them hook, line, and sinker. If you didn't have Beatles hair and Beatles songs, you were nowhere."

Berryhill was still only 17 years old when The Surfaris returned home from the Australia tour.

"To be a has-been at seventeen is pretty tough," he said.

In 1963, The Surfaris had signed a three-year contract with Decca Records, a five-album deal plus several singles.

According to Berryhill, the group's best album was produced by A&R (artists and repertoire) man Charles "Bud" Dant, *The Surfaris Play,* which was released in 1963. The band then recorded *Fun City, Hit City 64,* and *Hit City 65*.

"After Bud turned us over to Decca's new A&R man, Gary Usher, things went down fast," said Berryhill. "He wanted us to become a Beach Boys clone band. That forced us into an all-vocal format, doing cover songs from the late-'60s groups who were on the way up."

That resulted in what Berryhill calls the band's worst album, *It Ain't Me, Babe.*

"The title was fitting because a number of the tracks and song selections were not us," said Berryhill. "Usher didn't like our instrumental music but used our name to further his career rather than help us progress and build on the original sound we had created."

According to Berryhill, the surf music that was so popular before the British Invasion became a stigma for The Surfaris.

"We couldn't advance either. We started with *Wipe Out* and if you've seen the six original albums that we've done, you can see how we progressed from an all-instrumental band to an all-vocal band."

What didn't die was "Wipe Out" and the legacy that it has left for more than 50 years.

"'Wipe Out' is an iconic piece of Americana. The song itself has a life of its own. My publisher calls it the 'Wipe Out Industry.' I know that it started out in surf music and it's considered an iconic part of surf music. But whenever it's played, it brings a warmth to people's hearts," said Berryhill.

The original The Surfaris stayed together only until August 1965, when Connolly departed. He has since left the music business. Fuller left in 1966 and formed his own band, Jim Fuller and the Beatnik. He died on March 3, 2017. Wilson released an album of his own songs in 1987, then died on May 12, 1989. Pash died of heart failure in 2005.

Only Berryhill remains to carry on the legacy of The Surfaris, which is now a family band that includes his wife, Gene, and sons, Deven and Joel.

"I'm the last one playing. And we play 'Wipe Out' as our finale song and people stand up and they cheer. People will stand in line for an hour after the shows at the merch table to tell me their stories about how much 'Wipe Out' meant to them," said Berryhill. "I have fought lawsuit after lawsuit to protect The Surfaris' name and 'Wipe Out' because it is that important to me. When I play the stuff it's authentic, as I sound like The Surfaris without any special effort. I still don't want to change into a progressive surf band or any other band. It was our unique creation and part of who I am as a musician and part of surf music history."

Discography

The Surfaris

"Wipe Out"

Released 1963

Side 1

1 Wipe Out (2:12) - Bob Berryhill, Pat Connolly, Jim Fuller, Ron Wilson
2 Wiggle Wiggle (2:40)
3 Torquay (2:27) - George Tomsco
4 You Can't Sit Down (4:15) - Dee Clark, Kal Mann, Cornell Muldrow
5 Green Onions (2:45) - Booker T. Jones, Steve Cropper, Lewie Steinberg, Al Jackson, Jr.
6 Tequila (2:05) - Joe Johnson

Side 2

1 Wild Weekend (2:33) - Tom Shannon, Phil Todaro
2 Teen Beat (3:10) - Arthur Egnoian, Sandy Nelson
3 Yep! (2:45) - Duane Eddy, Lee Hazlewood
4 Memphis (2:52) - Chuck Berry
5 Surfer Joe (2:20) - Ron Wilson
6 Walk, Don't Run (2:09) - Johnny Smith

Something told them they were into something good

SELF-TITLED
Herman's Hermits
(1965)

Peter Noone didn't think anybody in England knew about what came to be called the British Invasion that was happening in the United States in the mid-1960s.

"We just knew that if you had an accent and you went on the television in America, you were in," said Noone.

So when the Beatles — who were eventually joined by other pop and rock music acts from the United Kingdom like the Dave Clark Five, the Kinks, the Animals, and the Rolling Stones — kicked open the door and exposed U.S. audiences to British music and culture, Noone and his group, Herman's Hermits, were ready to join the party.

"First of all, most of those bands from England were overeducated for the position. I think we were all much smarter than we appeared. We were able to do those interviews in America. We thought everybody was terribly polite," said Noone.

"If you see interviews with Elvis, they were putting him on the spot all the time. But the Beatles changed that. They were cheeky. They had no respect for the journalists. So that opened it up for us. The Beatles were charming, musically brilliant, funny, and attractive in every kind of way. Everybody in America thought that all English people were going to be like that," said Noone.

Second verse, same as the first. With Peter Noone on lead vocals, "I'm Henery the Eighth, I Am," an old British music hall song written in 1910 by Fred Murray and R.P. Weston, would be the second No. 1 single for Herman's Hermits. (Photo by Mike Morsch)

With the Beatles taking America by storm in February 1964 and laying the foundation for other British groups, Herman's Hermits would capitalize and have a huge year in 1965. Releasing their first album, the self-titled *Herman's Hermits* in February 1965, the group would eventually surpass the Beatles as the top-selling pop group in the U.S. that year.

It was a hectic existence for the band, which included Noone, who was only 15 years old at the time, on lead vocals; Derek "Lek" Leckenby on lead guitar; Barry Whitwam on drums; Karl Green on bass guitar; and Keith Hopwood on rhythm guitar and backing vocals.

The group's first single, "I'm Into Something Good," was released in August 1964 and went to No. 1 in the UK and No. 13 on the U.S. Billboard Hot 100 Singles chart. The band followed that up in short order with three more Top 5 singles in the first three months of 1965: "Can't You Hear My Heartbeat," which rose to No. 2 on the U.S. Billboard Singles charts; a cover of "Silhouettes," which had been recorded by the Rays, the Diamonds, and the Four Seasons, that got to No. 5 in the U.S.; and "Mrs. Brown You've Got a Lovely Daughter," which became the group's first No. 1 single in the U.S.

All of those singles would be on the *Herman's Hermits* album, which would be released in June 1965 and make it to No. 16 on the UK Albums chart and No. 2 on the U.S. Billboard 200 Albums chart.

There were actually two versions of the album, one released in the United Kingdom and a different one in the United States. There are some different songs on each album, and there were three different covers on the U.S. version.

"Before that first single came out, we were playing all the places in Liverpool that the Beatles had played before they made it," said Noone. "And we were very fortunate because we were different from all the other bands. We got lots of work; we were busy."

So busy that the band had an aggressive live show schedule. Once the band's first few singles charted, Herman's Hermits were in even more demand. They played all the dates that were scheduled before they became popular, and also new dates that were added because of that popularity. In between, they made records.

"Sometimes we would get in the van after a gig in the north of England, drive all night, and get into the studio at six in the morning. Because we were kids and enthusiastic, nobody ever complained," said Noone. "People used to sleep at different times in the van. We all couldn't sleep at the same time. We'd get to the studio early in the morning and The Animals would be packing up their gear and putting it into their van to go and do their thing. It all seemed perfectly natural."

The *Herman's Hermits* album would be recorded at Kingsway Studios in London. It was in the basement of the Midland Bank. The bank's old vault had been transformed into a recording studio.

The group had agreed to use Mickie Most — who had produced The Animals' first single "Baby Let Me Take You Home" and their follow-up single "The House of the Rising Sun," which became an international hit in 1964 — as their producer. In addition, Herman's Hermits had signed with EMI's Columbia label in Europe, and MGM Records in the U.S.

"We asked Mickie, 'Can we do what they [The Animals] did?' It was an inspiration to use him to be good because the stuff that Mickie had just recorded was going to number one," said Noone.

According to Noone, though, Herman's Hermits didn't have enough songs for the first album. In reality, they had enough songs; they just didn't have the right songs.

In that era, bands often recorded the repertoire of songs that they played live. The Beatles had recorded their repertoire, as did the Rolling Stones and the Dave Clark Five, from their live gigs in the London area.

"So we had all these songs that we did, but we couldn't record them if the Beatles had recorded them," said Noone. "We couldn't do 'Roll Over Beethoven' for example. There were all these songs that we knew, but we chose not to record them because somebody else has already recorded them. We needed different songs from the other bands, so we were looking for odd songs."

One of those "odd" songs was "Mrs. Brown You've Got a Lovely Daughter," written by Trevor Peacock, an English stage and television actor, screenwriter, and songwriter. It was originally sung by Tom Courtenay in 1963 in a British TV play called *The Lads* and also released as a single on UK Decca Records.

"Keith [Hopwood] had a guitar that was called the Gretsch Country Gentleman. A Chet Atkins style. And it had a damper on it that sounded like a banjo. It was designed to do that, make the guitar sound like a banjo. So he turned it up and it dampened the strings," said Noone. "And we were looking for a song on which to use that. We knew the guy who wrote the song, we knew the guy who sang it, and we learned it and started to do it on stage. And it had a kind of surreal effect on the audience. People would stop talking and go, 'What was that?' It's an odd sound. And it became part of our show."

When it came time to record it, the band did it in just two takes, using two microphones. According to Noone, the band also deliberately emphasized their English accents during the recording session.

"Mrs. Brown You've Got a Lovely Daughter" would go on the *Herman's Hermits* album and would be nominated for two Grammy Awards in 1965. But the band didn't initially see it as a single off the album.

"We didn't want them [record company officials] to release 'Mrs. Brown.' We thought it would hurt our career because it was such a novelty thing. It was OK live, but we didn't want it to be a single. We wanted 'Silhouettes' to be the next single," said Noone. "We thought we knew all about what other kids wanted. The thing about Herman's Hermits at that time was that we really were a boy band. We had a big operation but with no plans. We never could plan anything."

According to Noone, in that regard, the band was more like the Sex Pistols than the Beatles.

"We'd run in and make singles to get the record out by Thursday because a week from then, something else was going to happen," said Noone. "We were always looking over our shoulders to see who was going to be the next Herman's Hermits. So we just kept making records."

Indeed they did. Between August 1964 and September 1967, Herman's Hermits released 19 singles, 14 of which made the Top 20 on the U.S. Billboard Hot 100 Singles chart. Ten of those were Top 10 singles, with two of those reaching No. 1 in the U.S.

The second No. 1 single for Herman's Hermits would be another "odd" song, "I'm Henery the Eighth, I Am," an old British music hall song written in 1910 by Fred Murray and R.P. Weston. The song would also appear on the band's debut album, but only on the U.K. version.

"Everybody's grandfather in England knew that song, and there was a guy named Harry Champion who sang it," said Noone. "So Harry Champion came to Manchester and my grandfather took me to see him. I must have been four or five years old. He did a show and everybody sang along with the song."

The Herman's Hermits version of the song has an adlib in it from Noone though, that he didn't think would make it into the final recording of the song.

"When I say, 'Second verse, same as the first,' I just threw that in, meaning that the band would play the chorus again," said Noone. "Not that I was going to sing the second verse; just that OK, let's do the same thing again, thinking that would be deleted from the take," said Noone. "But it wasn't."

Being in the middle of the British Invasion brought worldwide attention to Noone and Herman's Hermits at a young age. And the music that they and the other British groups from that era made has stood the test of time.

"I think the music was good, but it was kind of naive in a way. The turning point with the Beatles was when they discovered Bob Dylan and decided that they could be hip. Before then, it was all beautiful love songs. But the Beatles stopped writing those pop songs," said Noone. "They stopped writing those songs that everybody in the family could get a piece of. And they never went back. But their records that sell are just simple and fresh."

Noone believes that was because in England during the 1960s, nearly everyone came from a musical family.

"I can remember the terror of going to my grandmother's house. My dad had a trombone, my grandfather and auntie who lived there played the piano, my Uncle Lawrence played the trumpet and my grandmother sang these horrible soprano songs. And it would go round and round," said Noone. "And everybody's house that I went to, there was a cool guy who lived around the corner who had a guitar. That made him kind of unusual. It was new. Everybody had somebody in the house who liked music or played music."

Herman's Hermits started to fade in the late 1960s and Noone eventually left the group in 1971. There have been different iterations of the band over the years and Noone, himself, has toured as a solo act for decades and continues to tour.

"I still work on the joy of the music that I had as a teenager and I hope that the audience gets that. I'm onstage and I really believe that I'm seventeen," said Noone. "Sometimes during the songs I get to where I become the character that I want to be. But now, when this old geezer sings about Mrs. Brown's daughter, there is a bit of Chester the Molester in it for me."

Noone hopes that today's audiences can still see the joy that he experiences when performing the music that's now been around for about 50 years.

"I look in the audience and I see all these sixty-year-old blokes and I go, 'They must be really happy that we're still enthusiastic.' You go and see these oldies bands and it just seems to be that they're still enthusiastic," said Noone. "I'm fortunate. I say it onstage and people laugh when I say it, but I love my songs. I finish my songs and I say, 'Oh, that felt good.' And there are different ones that I enjoy on different nights.

"And I think that's part of it. There was a period of massive optimism and enthusiasm in the 1960s. When I think about Herman's Hermits, I think about our band — there we were in our van, thinking we could make it. And our competition was the Beatles. We should have quit," he said.

Discography

Herman's Hermits

Self-titled

Released (US - Feb. 13, 1965; UK - September 1965)

UK version

Side one

1. Heartbeat (2:52) Bob Montgomery, Norman Petty
2.Travellin' Light (2:36) Sid Tepper, Roy C. Bennett
3. I'll Never Dance Again (3:30) Barry Mann, Mike Anthony
4. Walkin' with My Angel (2:24) Gerry Goffin, Carole King
5. Dream On (2:07) Gary Gordon
6. I Wonder (2:10) Johnny Pearson

Side two

1. For Your Love 2:28 Graham Gouldman
2. Don't Try to Hurt Me (2:08) Keith Hopwood
3. Tell Me Baby (2:16) Derek Leckenby, Keith Hopwood
4. I'm Henery VIII, I Am (1:53) Fred Murray, Robert Patrick Weston
5. The End of the World (3:05) Arthur Kent, Sylvia Dee
6. Mrs. Brown, You've Got a Lovely Daughter (2:48) Trevor Peacock

US version

Side one

1. **I'm into Something Good (2:31) Gerry Goffin, Carole King**
2. **Mrs. Brown, You've Got a Lovely Daughter (2:46) Trevor Peacock**
3. **Kansas City Loving (2:07) Jerry Leiber and Mike Stoller**
4. **I Wonder (2:06) Johnny Pearson**
5. **Sea Cruise (2:08) Huey Piano Smith**
6. **Walking with My Angel (2:19) Goffin, King**

Side two

1. **Show Me Girl (2:34) Goffin, King**
2. **I Understand (Just How You Feel) (2:58) Pat Best**
3. **Mother-in-Law (2:21) Allen Toussaint**
4. **Your Hand in Mine (2:00) Charles Silverman, Harvey Lisberg**
5. **I Know Why (2:03) Charles Silverman, Derek Leckenby**
6. **Thinking of You (2:03) Johnny Pearson**

From the basement to the penthouse

KIND OF A DRAG

The Buckinghams

(1967)

When the Buckinghams first formed, people often referred to them as a garage band. But they were actually a basement band.

The members — Carl Giammarese, Nick Fortuna, Dennis Tufano, John Poulos, and Dennis Miccolis — would rehearse in the basements of their parents' homes. When one set of parents got tired of listening to them after a week, they'd get kicked out and have to go to the next guy's parents' house.

One evening in 1966, they were working up a song in the basement of the Giammarese household.

"I remember my mother came down and said, 'It's really a catchy tune. That might be a great song.' We were like, 'Yeah, that's cool,' not thinking at all about the magnitude of it," said Giammarese.

Although they continued to develop the song, they didn't give Mrs. Giammarese's opinion of it much more thought.

Originally calling themselves the Pulsations, they first attracted the attention of Carl Bonafede, a local disc jockey who was spinning records at the Holiday Ballroom in Chicago. The Holiday Ballroom was owned by Dan Belloc, and he, too, had taken note of the Pulsations.

"Belloc got interested in the band because he noticed right away that no matter who played there, people would dance and have a good time. But when we played, people would stop and come to the front of the stage and watch. He thought, 'These guys got something special,'" said Giammarese.

With Bonafede assuming the role of the band's manager, and with the support of Belloc, they landed the group a contract with WGN-TV in Chicago to appear on *All-Time Hits*, a musical variety show that ran for 13 weeks on the station.

According to the September 15, 1965 edition of the *Chicago Tribune*, Larry Wolters wrote about the show: "So some of you missed *The Fugitive* and a feature movie last night on the networks to see the new *All-Time Hits* on WGN-TV. Worth it, wasn't it? Good, durable, melodic music — music that people love. The 9 to 10 pm show was a happy addition to the regular fare of TV violence. Bob Carroll was a treat as singing host. Also great was Billy Williams, singer on so many Sid Caesar shows. Also on hand were Bob Newkirk of the Breakfast Club, Doree Crews, and the Joe Eich Singers, Bob Trendler's band, and The Buckinghams, folk singers."

"We were the Pulsations up until then and the show liked the group but didn't like the name," said Giammarese. "So somebody who worked for the show came up with The Buckinghams. They were looking for something to capitalize on the British Invasion. We said, yeah, that's cool. So we started doing the show as The Buckinghams."

The exposure that The Buckinghams got from *All-Time Hits* increased the band's regional popularity and resulted in a contract with USA Records, a Chicago-based label founded in 1960 by record distributor Jim Golden. Its office was right across the street from Chess Records at 2120 S. Michigan Avenue. The studio was notable at the time because the Rolling Stones had recorded an instrumental called "2120 South Michigan Avenue" that was released on the band's

Dennis Tufano, lead singer on "Kind of a Drag," said the song evolved as The Buckinghams continued to rehearse it, primarily on the placement of the backing vocal lyrics.
(Photo by Mike Morsch)

"5 x 5" extended-play record, and eventually included on the Stones' second album, *12 x 5*, released in October 1964.

It was at the Chess Records studio that The Buckinghams would record some of the band's cover material that it had had been doing in its live show. Songs included "I'll Go Crazy" by James Brown; "I Call Your Name" by John Lennon and Paul McCartney; and "I've Been Wrong," a Hollies song given to the group by Hollies member Graham Nash.

WLS-AM 890 radio was supportive of local bands in those days and had given these cover songs some airplay in regular rotation. That gave The Buckinghams a lot of exposure throughout the Midwest.

Still, the band was looking for something more.

"None of us were songwriters, but we still wanted an original song," said Giammarese.

Bonafede approached Jim Holvay, another singer-songwriter in the Chicago area who had first been in a band called the Executives, and later in a band called the Mob, to ask if he had a song for The Buckinghams.

"So Jim Holvay threw this song down with him strumming on an electric guitar that wasn't even plugged in. He strummed it out for Bonafede, who had brought a tape player to make a recording of it, and Bonafede brought it to us," said Giammarese.

The song was called "Kind of a Drag." And that was the song that Giammarese's mother heard the band working up that evening in her basement.

"We were like, well, it's got a catchy thing to it. 'Kind of a drag' — everybody uses that term," said Giammarese.

Belloc, who was also a big band leader, had put some horns on the previously recorded songs "I'll Go Crazy" and "I Call Your Name" and thought that "Kind of a Drag" also needed horns.

"Belloc said, 'You know, we need to dress this track up. We need to put horns on it.' I can't remember exactly who came up with the intro for it, it might have been our keyboard player at the time, but I'm not exactly sure how we put that together," said Giammarese. "It was sort of a regal entrance for the song. A real big beginning, which was a hook itself. Then of course, the first line grabbed you. So the song had all the elements that we needed."

According to lead singer Tufano, the song evolved as The Buckinghams continued to rehearse it, primarily on the placement of the backing vocal lyrics, which were "Listen to me when I'm speaking cause you know the words I'm thinking," as well as "And I know that you've been cheating, oh, I hope that we'll be meeting."

"That part was actually another section of the song, like a B section of the song when Jim [Holvay] handed it to us. And it just wasn't feeling right; it was just elongated," said Tufano. "So when we were in rehearsals one day, I said when I sing the bridge part, what if we put that underneath it to save the time. And it laid in perfectly, like it was made for the song. And it became one of the hooks of the song, because people had to lean in to listen to it. People started asking, 'Hey, what are they singing in the background?' And it became a more of mystery, which was great. That added to the essence of the hit."

After rehearsing and getting the song where they wanted it, The Buckinghams went back into the studio at Chess Records to record the basic track and the vocals.

But USA Records just sat on the song for a while. Once the label did release it, though, WLS started playing it and it took off.

By February 1967, "Kind of a Drag" was No. 1 on the U.S. Billboard Hot 100 Singles chart, knocking The Monkees' "I'm a Believer" out of the top spot.

"I don't think any of us had a sense of the magnitude of 'Kind of a Drag.' We liked the song and we thought it was a cool tune. We thought that it had a chance, that it had legs, that it was gonna do something for us. But I don't think any of us realized that it was going to be that big of a hit and pass the Rolling Stones and The Monkees," said Giammarese.

"After that, to be honest, if we had been on Columbia Records from the get-go, it could have been even a bigger hit. We wasted a lot of time," said Giammarese. "Right after we recorded that record, we had fired our keyboard player, Dennis Miccolis, and we were in search of a new keyboard player. We got one guy temporarily for a while that didn't work out."

According to Giammarese, USA Records had independent distribution and was working with a lot of different distributors. Giammarese believes that the label had a difficult time keeping up with the orders for the record.

The Buckinghams also didn't have a national agency at the time. The Willard Alexander Booking Agency was booking the band, but Giammarese said the agency missed the boat by not getting the band on any TV shows outside Chicago.

"So our opportunities with that record came and went. We were a bunch of kids who made mistakes along the way, but one thing we realized collectively was that if we were going to keep this thing going and not become one-hit wonders, we needed to connect with somebody who could take us to the next level, which included a booking agency and a record company that could do better things for us," said Giammarese.

That approach made them some enemies in their hometown.

"All these people were coming down on us. 'You're never gonna get your record played again if you leave us.' We were worried, but we also knew that we didn't want to become the Cryan' Shames or the American Breed [other local bands] with one hit. We wanted to take it further."

Enter James William Guercio, former bassist and road manager for Chad and Jeremy, and also a Chicago guy. Guercio — who would go on a few years later to produce some of the band Chicago's early albums — had connections in Los Angeles with Columbia Records and the William Morris Booking Agency. And The Buckinghams' contract with USA Records had run out.

"When you have the number one record in the country, it's not that hard to get a record deal when you're in that position. So that was no-brainer," said Giammarese.

The Buckinghams had been in the studio on and off recording singles and had accumulated enough songs for USA Records that by the time they left the label and went to Columbia, they had enough material to put together an album.

Released in 1967, it was also called *Kind of a Drag,* and would feature that hit, along with "I'll Go Crazy," "I Call Your Name," and "I've Been Wrong." The 14-song album also included “I’m A Man,” written by Bo Diddley, and “Lawdy Miss Clawdy,” written by Lloyd Price.

Columbia released “Lawdy Miss Clawdy” as the follow-up single to “Kind of a Drag,” and The Buckinghams then recorded a new single called “Don’t You Care.” All three songs charted at the same time.

With Columbia’s backing, 1967 became a magical year for The Buckinghams.

“We were on the road a lot. We played three hundred dates that year. Guercio kept setting up studio time and we’d fly into New York and do a whirlwind session, and then we’d go back out on the road and start playing again,” said Giammarese. “We would just do the basic tracks and the vocals, and then they put on strings and horns and mixed it. And the hits just kept coming.”

The singles chart was dotted with songs by The Buckinghams in 1967. “Lawdy Miss Clawdy” reached No. 41 and “Don’t You Care” made it to No. 6. That was followed by “Mercy, Mercy, Mercy,” No. 5 on both Billboard and Cashbox; “Hey Baby (They’re Playing Our Song),” No. 12 on Billboard and No. 5 on Cashbox; and “Susan,” No. 11 on Billboard and No. 7 on Cashbox.

“It was pretty exciting. In 1966 and 1967, things were really starting to blossom as far as the changing ’60s music scene,” said Tufano. “There were a lot of bands coming out at that time and we were at the forefront of it. It was like somebody planted the seeds in the early ’60s and these things started to grow pretty fast. It just kept going.

“There were so many bands, and yet everybody was able to play their music. Nobody was cancelled out. There was enough running room for everyone to have their songs out there, which was great because most of the shows we did back in the ’60s, there were five acts. And every act had a hit record. It was pretty powerful stuff,” said Tufano.

"You'd pinch yourself, but you didn't have a lot of time to think about it because you were so busy. I thought about it more years later. You're on the go playing gigs and recording and doing a lot of interviews and some TV shows and a lot of teen magazine stuff," said Giammarese. "It was kind of scary, to tell you the truth. I hadn't really been out that much. I grew up in a household that never took their kids out to dinner. We always ate at home; we never ate in restaurants. And then I was getting exposed to dances and playing gigs and eating in restaurants and then here we were doing it on a national level."

Giammarese believes that although being on a national stage was intimidating, what made it easier for him was that The Buckinghams were a close-knit group that went through it all together and drew support from each other.

"We felt that we fit in with the pop music that was going on at the time. AM radio was still very big and our peers that were making hits alongside us, like the Turtles and Gary Puckett and Tommy James, we felt we were at that level. We weren't a bubblegum band, but we were definitely a pop group that was making pop-sounding records," he said.

"We were constantly on the move and at twenty years old, you've got all the energy in the world you need," said Tufano. "We were so excited. And then having the actual experience of fans and having people screaming for you. It was a little mystifying. But the energy level was so high, I think that's what kept us going. We were always buzzed by this acceptance."

The band was also oblivious to what was going on in the world at the time, like the Vietnam War.

"We didn't pay a lot of attention to it. Our songs were basically love songs, making up, not breaking up, songs. There was no heavy message in any of our music. It was just nice, fairly easygoing love songs, really," said Giammarese.

By 1969, though, Giammarese believed the band was losing touch with the rest of the music industry. Radio had changed, seemingly overnight. Pop music on AM stations was becoming less popular than hard rock and roll and commercial success was starting to come to bands who were getting more airplay on FM stations. The Monterey Pop Festival and Woodstock came along. Jimi Hendrix and Janis Joplin had emerged, as did more underground hippie groups.

"By 1970, we were a little bit passé and unable to change our image. It was what it was. We tried a little bit with an album called *Portraits* that we spent a lot of time on. That was like our *Sgt. Pepper*. But people weren't buying it. Those that were still fans wanted to hear 'Kind of a Drag' and 'Don't You Care.' The new audience wasn't responding to it," he said.

The band revamped a bit, tried to portray a different image and released some singles. But by that time, Columbia was losing interest and so were the band members.

And trouble with management helped accelerate the band's eventual demise.

"We were flowing pretty good. But the management collapsed on us. And it took us out of the game," said Tufano. "It seemed like The Buckinghams were in a Ferrari flying down the musical highway and then all of a sudden they fell off the edge of the earth. That's because we had litigation problems with management, money was missing; it was pretty much the same story with a lot of the bands."

When The Buckinghams broke up in 1970, Giammarese and Tufano stayed together as a singer-songwriting duo. They wanted to go in a different direction with their music and started playing clubs around Chicago.

They did attract the attention of Lou Adler, who had founded Ode Records, which included Carole King and Cheech & Chong in its stable of artists. King was just coming off a No. 1 album with *Tapestry* in early 1971.

The duo's first album, titled *Tufano & Giammarese*, one of three albums they would record for Ode Records, attracted modest attention, but it wasn't enough.

"It didn't happen for us. We did three albums with Adler in the 1970s. I have to say, Lou Adler gave us a great opportunity and we didn't come through with any hits. We just weren't writing the hits. It was our fault," said Giammarese.

Another challenge was that Adler just didn't have a comparable act to pair with the duo. Tufano & Giammarese spent a year opening for Cheech & Chong.

"I'm telling you, it was torture. Don't get me wrong, I have a lot of respect for those guys. They were perfectly in tune with what was going on at the time. But their audience was a whole bunch of dopers," said Giammarese. "And then here's Dennis and I doing this light acoustic music. So we'd open for them and sometimes we wouldn't go over. And Tommy Chong would complain to Lou, saying, 'Hey those guys are bumming out our audience.' And then when we went over well, he would complain we were taking away from them. We couldn't win. But Lou didn't have anywhere to put us. He wanted us to tour. But Ode Records was such a small label there was just nobody to tour with. Carole King would have been perfect for us, but Carole wouldn't tour at the time. She was very introverted and didn't want to perform live."

After the three albums, Tufano and Giammarese split up. Tufano remained in California to pursue an acting career and Giammarese returned to Chicago.

"In 1970 when The Buckinghams broke up, there was no interest at all in our music. But then the 1980s came along and everything became the 1960s again," said Giammarese. "All of a sudden the baby boomers, who were still relatively young then, came out of the woodwork. I think it had a lot to do with that they wanted to hear their music again; they were still young enough to go out and enjoy our music and have fun and party. And they were established where they had some money to spend. All those things came together."

The Buckinghams, now with original members Giammarese and Fortuno, joined the "Happy Together Tour" and are once again playing to sold-out audiences. Over the years, the "Happy Together Tour" has featured the Turtles, The Association and the Cowsills, among others.

Tufano also appears as a solo act in shows featuring bands from the 1960s that are still performing to packed houses.

"We couldn't have had better material to go out there and play," said Tufano about the early years of The Buckinghams. "I can still sing those songs from my heart with real emotion and meaning. When I grab the microphone now, I'm nineteen again.

"When interviewers would ask me back in the 1960s how long we thought we were going to be doing this, I was like, I don't know, for a little while, as long as we can. I expected it to last a couple of years and then move on," said Giammarese. "But now I get younger people that will come up to me at a show and say my parents played your records so I'm familiar with them. And that's cool."

Discography

The Buckinghams
"Kind of a Drag"
Released 1967

1. I'll Go Crazy (2:06) James Brown
2. Don't Want to Cry (2:11)
3. Virginia Wolf (2:30)
4. Beginner's Love (1:54)
5. Sweets for My Sweet (2:07) Doc Pomus / Mort Shuman
6. I've Been Wrong (1:54)
7. I Call Your Name (2:10) John Lennon / Paul McCartney
8. Makin' up and Breakin' Up (2:11) Jimmy Holvay
9. You Make Me Feel So Good (2:37) Chris White
10. Summertime (3:54) George Gershwin / Ira Gershwin / DuBose Heyward
11. Love Ain't Enough (2:10)
12. Kind of a Drag (2:07) Jimmy Holvay
13. Lawdy Miss Claudy (2:01) Lloyd Price
14. I'm a Man (5:12) Bo Diddley

Flying high with a hit two years later

ALBUM 1700

Peter, Paul and Mary
(1967)

By 1965, Chad Mitchell, who had co-founded the folk music group the Chad Mitchell Trio in 1959, had decided to leave the band and pursue a solo career. A young and previously unknown singer/songwriter named John Denver emerged from the band's audition process, replaced Mitchell and started to write songs for the group.

Early in Denver's tenure, the group was backstage preparing for a show when Denver brought one of his new compositions to the band members to see what they thought.

"I thought it was a terrific song. All you have to do is listen to John's music. He always had a way of putting words together so that you got it immediately," said Paul Prestopino, a featured guitarist with the Chad Mitchell Trio who had joined the group in 1962 when the three featured singers were Mitchell, Mike Kobluk, and Joe Frazier.

"There are good songs out there where it takes a few listenings before you really latch onto where it's going. And there are other songs that are so simplistic that they go through your head like water. And then there are the ones where it's really a nice constructed lyric that tells the story and paints the pictures and you get it," said Prestopino.

"And this was a wonderful song because you get the story and the emotion simultaneously on first listen."

The musical director for the Chad Mitchell Trio was Milton Okun, a producer, arranger, and conductor who had been with the group from its inception. Okun was the founder of Cherry Lane Music Publishing Company, Inc., and also happened to be the musical director for Peter, Paul and Mary.

Denver took it to Okun and the musical director liked it. But he didn't like the title that Denver had chosen for the song: "Oh, Babe, I Hate to Go."

According to Prestopino, Okun told Denver that he should change the title to "Leaving on a Jet Plane."

"I think these things just came out of John and then he was on to the next thing," said Prestopino. "I think he liked the song; I think he thought it was good because he wouldn't have gathered us around backstage to hear it. And we all liked it."

The Chad Mitchell Trio performed "Leaving on a Jet Plane" live for the first time in 1966 at the Cellar Door in Washington, D.C. after Denver had replaced Mitchell. The song would be recorded by the Chad Mitchell Trio in 1967, and also by Spanky and Our Gang that same year.

Early in Denver's tenure with the Chad Mitchell Trio, Okun and Denver became close and Okun became the publisher of Denver's songs.

Also in 1967, Peter, Paul and Mary were heading into the studio for rehearsals on the songs that would go on their seventh studio album, titled *Album 1700.* The name was chosen because its original LP issue was Warner Brothers Records catalog number "W-1700" for the mono version and "WS-1700" for the stereo version.

"At some point during rehearsals, Milt played 'Leaving on a Jet Plane' for Mary Travers, who fell in love

Paul Prestopino, a featured guitarist with the Chad Mitchell Trio who had joined the group in 1962, said that it was producer Milt Okun who convinced songwriter John Denver to change the name of his song "Oh Babe, I Hate to Go" before Okun pitched it to Peter, Paul and Mary. (Photo by Phil McAuliffe)

Peter Yarrow said that at some point during rehearsals, Milt Okun played "Leaving on a Jet Plane" for Mary Travers, who fell in love with the song. And based on her enthusiasm for it, Peter, Paul and Mary recorded it for their *Album 1700* in 1967.
(Photo by Phil McAuliffe)

with the song," said Peter Yarrow. "And based on her enthusiasm for it, we went ahead and recorded it."

It was not the first Denver song that Peter, Paul and Mary had recorded. A year earlier, Okun had brought Denver's song "For Bobbie," which Travers changed to "For Baby," to the group. The three of them liked the song and recorded it for the group's sixth studio album, *The Peter, Paul and Mary Album,* released in 1966.

"John was starting to write. I know the song that Mary Travers recorded as 'For Baby,' he originally wrote as 'For Bobbie.' Bobbie was a young woman by the name of Bobbie Wargo, who was a college student in Columbia, Missouri," said Prestopino. "She was John's girlfriend. That fell apart not long afterwards. I know nothing of the specifics nor do I really care. But that song 'For Bobbie' was written for Bobbie Wargo and then Mary heard it, changed it to 'For Baby,' and changed a couple of words to make it work for a parent singing to a young child."

Peter, Paul and Mary would go with another Denver song on *Album 1700,* which would be released in March 1967. But "Leaving on a Jet Plane," which would become Peter, Paul and Mary's most successful and final hit, wouldn't gain any traction as a hit single until 1969.

According to Yarrow, he, Travers, and Noel Paul Stookey didn't choose which of their songs would be released as singles. The executives at Warner Brothers Records made those decisions.

"It wasn't until there was a spontaneous excitement around 'Leaving on a Jet Plane' at certain radio stations that Warner Brothers thought of it as a potential single. And that was two years after the album had been released," said Yarrow. "And frankly, that happened on more than one occasion. That happened with 'Puff the Magic Dragon' on our second album [*Moving,* released in January 1963]. It was not recognized at all as a potential single until one radio station started playing and it got extraordinary response.

"That pattern existed a good deal in those days, where it was a disc jockey or music director that would hear a song and say, 'That's a hit and I'm going to play it.' And that would impact the evolution and outcome of a song," said Yarrow.

Album 1700 would reach No. 15 on the U.S. Billboard Pop Albums chart and would hang around for nearly two years. When "Leaving on a Jet Plane" was finally released as a single by Warner Brothers Records, it became No. 1 on the U.S. Billboard Hot 100 Singles chart, the U.S. Billboard Easy Listening chart, and the U.S. Cash Box Top 100 chart.

"I thought it was a special song. I thought it was special in terms of all the songs we did for that album. But I wasn't thinking about hit or no hit; it was just a great song," said Yarrow. "It wasn't as if we didn't sometimes say, 'This is going to be a hit.' We did, particularly with 'Blowin' in the Wind.' We knew it with our heart of hearts. But that was seldom the case. We simply would love the songs and choose them based on the track record of the writer. And that's why some of the writers of songs that we recorded were unknown. We didn't look for a hit-writing writer and then say let's record that song and hope we get a hit. We just never needed to do that."

Album 1700 also contained another song that was a little different from what Peter, Paul and Mary had done before, but according to Yarrow, the group was at a point where it was experimenting with its music.

"I Dig Rock and Roll Music" was written by Stookey, James Mason, and Dave Dixon. The lyrics refer to the rock artists of the era, specifically the Beatles, The Mamas & The Papas, and Donovan.

According to Stookey in previously published reports, his work with Mason and Dixon was one of the first times that he had collaborated with songwriters other than Yarrow.

"Noel wrote 'I Dig Rock and Roll Music' and presented it to the table. And even though it was very much different than most of the songs that we were recording, we were in the mode of experimenting a little bit," said Yarrow. "Phil Ramone at that point was an engineer for us and he really heard and understood the song and helped us bring it to the place where it became what it was on the album."

Yarrow, Stookey, and Travers had songwriting credits on eight of the 12 songs on *Album 1700.* One song, "Bob Dylan's Dream," was written by Dylan and already had a history of its own by 1967.

There are various published reports regarding the song's origins, written by Dylan in 1963, none of which appear to be conclusive.

One account theorizes that the song recalls the time Dylan spent in Greenwich Village with comedian friend Hugh Romney, in the early 1960s when Dylan's life was less complex. Another version, this one advanced by biographer Robert Shelton, suggests that the song is about the lost innocence of Dylan's adolescence in Hibbing, Minnesota.

According to Yarrow, he wanted to include the song on *Album 1700* because it held personal significance for him.

"'Bob Dylan's Dream' was very special to me because in my history with Bob, he had come to Woodstock and stayed at my cabin in the summer of 1963. And what we shared there at that time was really very well-characterized in that song," said Yarrow.

When it came time to shoot the photo for the cover of *Album 1700,* Peter, Paul and Mary decided not to experiment as much with the cover as they did with the music on the inside.

The photo shows the three, dressed as 1920s gangsters, standing in front of a car that's parked in front of a red brick house.

"We worked with Milton Glaser, a designer, and we came up with an idea. At the time, it was not unusual for performers to get into a costume and then pose. Not necessarily something in which they would appear in every day. It was a very lyrical time in that sense, where people would get dressed up in crazy clothes. That was just a fun thing," said Yarrow. "That was actually my car and we all dressed up like gangsters and Mary was the gun moll. The picture was taken in front of Noel's home in Greenwich Village."

In 1970, just a year after "Leaving on a Jet Plane" reached No. 1, Peter, Paul and Mary broke up to pursue solo careers. They reunited for concerts in 1972 and 1978, and then one more time in 1981. From that point, they essentially stayed together recording albums and playing approximately 45 shows a year until Travers' death in 2009.

Yarrow and Stookey still occasionally perform together, sometimes accompanied on guitar by Paul Prestopino of the Chad Mitchell Trio.

"For me, to be able to share with all the audiences makes me whole in my heart. You never know who is in the audience. You know you are only one person of many who are trying to do the same thing and you just go forward and do it," said Yarrow. "So to me, if I weren't able to do that in my life, the great gift of the legacy of Peter, Paul and Mary and Pete Seeger and the Weavers and Woody Guthrie would not be able to be carried on by me.

And that would a huge loss. That's really central to who I am and what I'm about."

Discography

Peter, Paul and Mary

"Album 1700"

Released March 18, 1967

Side 1

1. Rolling Home (3:31) Eric Andersen
2. Leaving on a Jet Plane (3:30) John Denver
3. Weep For Jamie (4:12) Peter Yarrow
4. No Other Name (2:31) Paul Stookey
5 The House Song (4:18) Paul Stookey, Robert Bannard
6. The Great Mandala The Wheel Of Life (4:45) Peter Yarrow

Side 2

1. I Dig Rock And Roll Music (2:33) Paul Stookey, James Mason, Dave Dixon
2. If I Had Wings (2:22) Peter Yarrow, Susan Yardley
3. I'm In Love With A Big Blue Frog (2:08) Leslie Braunstein
4. Whatshername (3:27) Paul Stookey, Dave Dixon, Richard Kniss
5. Bob Dylan's Dream (4:01) Bob Dylan
6. The Song Is Love (2:44) Dave Dixon, Richard Kniss, Paul Stookey, Peter Yarrow, Mary Travers

Sunday afternoon is the only time for significant others

GROOVIN'

The Young Rascals
(1967)

Musicians work primarily on Friday and Saturday nights. And the women in their lives, well, some don't like that too much.

That's the way it was in the mid-1960s for Felix Cavaliere of the Young Rascals. By the end of 1966, his band's self-titled debut album had reached No. 10 on the Cash Box Album chart and No. 15 on the Billboard Top 200 Albums chart. The record featured the group's first No. 1 single, "Good Lovin'" and positioned the band to begin writing and recording more of their own material.

It also created a demand for the Young Rascals, particularly on Friday and Saturday nights, much to the dismay of their wives and girlfriends.

"That's not exactly their cup of tea because, hey, you can understand when they say, 'What do I do while you're out there entertaining?' So it's a normal situation and any musician will tell you that they go through a lot of changes with that," said Cavaliere. "And so groovin' on a Sunday afternoon became the only time that we had together."

It also became the inspiration — along with Cavaliere's girlfriend at the time — for what would become the next No. 1 hit for the Young Rascals.

Felix Cavaliere co-wrote the title track "Groovin'" for the Young Rascals' third album, which was released in 1967. (Photo by Mike Morsch)

"Groovin'" was the title track from the band's third album, released in 1967. Written by Cavaliere and bandmate Eddie Brigati, the song reached No. 1 on the Billboard Hot 100 charts and stayed there for four weeks.

Cavaliere's girlfriend was a young woman named Adrienne Buccheri, and he believes that she served as a muse for him.

"That was the age where all of us were kind of like dating and getting engaged. That's what happened to me, basically. I fell madly in love with this woman who actually turned out to be a muse, no question about it," said Cavaliere. "That's really the only reason she was in my life. It was very strange. We were engaged, but never married. I really feel like she was like the old poetic muses. They just come into your life for a reason and spark that kind of emotion and feeling that generates those types of songs."

It was no coincidence then, given the relationship of Cavaliere and Buccheri at the time, that the next single off the *Groovin'* album to become a Top 5 single for the band was "How Can I Be Sure," which rose to No. 4 on the Billboard Hot 100 Singles chart.

"She was very young, much younger than I was, and it was totally crazy. It culminated in 'How Can I Be Sure.' I woke up one day and said, 'What the hell am I doing? I'm going out with a kid.' It was strange," said Cavaliere. "She ended up marrying a very dear friend of mine and they had a couple of children together; then unfortunately, she passed. That's the story. It's kind of strange, you know. I have to be careful with it now because my present-day wife doesn't like that story too much."

According to Cavaliere, the music business in the mid- to late-1960s was a singles-oriented world. Radio was based on the Top 40 and the challenge for bands of that era was to get airplay and get a hit single.

"It certainly wasn't easy with the competition that was out there, which was phenomenal," said Cavaliere. "But it also raised the bar to a high level, so a lot of music from that time is still here."

The band's label, Atlantic Records, ended up releasing eight of the 11 songs on *Groovin'* as A- or B-side singles. Cavaliere and Brigati co-wrote eight of the songs. Guitarist Gene Cornish wrote two, "I'm So Happy Now," which was the B-side of "How Can I Be Sure," and "I Don't Love You Anymore," one of the three songs that wasn't released as a single.

As was the case with many bands then, the pressure from the labels to continue to produce hit singles and albums was intense. Cavaliere and Brigati were well aware of that pressure.

"And the reason was because Atlantic was not a major label at that time, so money was an issue. Anytime you combine money with art, it's difficult," said Cavaliere. "So there was a lot of pressure from Atlantic to keep product going out. The other thing was, it was a challenge. But there was also a tremendous amount of good luck, good fortune, and being in the right place at the right time. Yes, you felt the pressure but you felt it from a different angle, from the people who were behind the label."

Despite that pressure, Cavaliere also admits that the environment in which Atlantic Records put the band was positive and helped contribute to the band's success.

"I always equate it as a very fertile type of land. All we had to do was pop a seed in there, man. And it grew, because the team that we had at our disposal was phenomenal," said Cavaliere.

While the Beatles had George Martin as producer, the Young Rascals had their own mentors, including Arif Mardin and Tom Dowd.

Mardin began his career with Atlantic Records in 1963 and quickly rose through the ranks becoming studio manager, label house producer, and arranger. Dowd was a recording engineer for Atlantic who frequently worked with Mardin at the label. The two of them, along with producer Jerry Wexler, were responsible for establishing what was called the Atlantic Sound in the 1960s.

Even though the Young Rascals are listed as producers on the *Groovin'* album, Mardin, Dowd, and Wexler were at the band's disposal during the recording of the album. "We won't see this type of talent around for many generations. They were brilliant, brilliant human beings in their own right," said Cavaliere. "Even though we were totally in charge of production on the albums, on the singles, the talent that was available to us in that room and the energy that was created by the constant zeal for perfection and for good music was incredible. I'm very, very lucky to have

Eddie Brigati co-wrote right of the songs that would appear on the *Groovin'* album for the Young Rascals. (Photo by Mike Morsch)

been involved in that. I have some friends who have been involved in the recording business for years and they didn't have the experience that I had. They didn't have this wonderful, amazing, friendly, happy, fun atmosphere. In that regard, Atlantic was a magic place."

According to Cavaliere, the Young Rascals exercised that control over their records from the get-go with Atlantic.

"What we had from Atlantic Records was unique in that we were completely in charge of production; every decision had to be approved by us. I demanded that when I went there because I really had an idea of what I wanted to do," said Cavaliere. "I said to the company, look, you liked what you heard when you signed us up. Give me a shot. And the good fortune that comes into the picture is Arif Mardin and Tom Dowd. Are you kidding? You couldn't have dreamt that. What a joy it was to make music in those days."

That type of creative freedom also was evident in the writing process for the songs on *Groovin',* according to Cavaliere. And although it was hard work, he and Brigati were in the groove during their writing sessions for *Groovin'*.

"There are two people writing these songs. I'm writing most of the music and the titles and themes. My partner was filling in the verse repartee. It wore him out, man, I'll be honest with you," said Cavaliere. "Music to me comes very natural. For me to sit down and write a song, it's pretty easy. So I was way ahead in terms of the music being before the lyrical content. If you look at this job that you have as a blessing, then that makes life easy. But if you look at this job as a J-O-B, it will wear you out. It didn't wear me out because I loved every moment of it and I mean that truthfully.

"As a writer, when you get a concept in your brain and then all of a sudden it manifests itself in a studio on speakers, it's beyond belief. How cool is that?"

Cavaliere said that he, Brigati, Cornish, and drummer Dino Danelli were all pretty happy when they heard the finished album; like they were for all the albums they created.

"We were always very proud of what we did. You walk out of the studio and certainly there were periods of turmoil within the organization during the recording. But we always walked out of there smiling, saying 'Wow!'"

"You also walk out of there pretty tired. It was a lot of time. And I was present for every second of it. We never mailed anything in. I was there for everything and I enjoyed every aspect of the process, from the creation of the songs to the recording of the track to the singing and the mixing, even to the mastering whenever possible. First of all, I wanted to learn, and second of all, that's your product. You gotta be there," he said. "I guess you always like it as a finished album, but you're apprehensive about whether other people are going to like it. And you're tired."

The apprehension about the *Groovin'* album turned out to be unfounded. Everybody liked it. The album reached No. 5 on the U.S. Billboard Top 200 Albums chart and No. 6 on the Cash Box Albums chart.

In addition to the album's title track making it to No. 1 and "How Can I Be Sure" getting to No. 4 on the singles chart, two other Brigati-Cavaliere collaborations, "A Girl Like You" and "You Better Run," reached No. 10 and No. 20 respectively on the U.S. Billboard Hot 100 Singles chart.

"The situation with *Groovin'* in those days, all of us were kind of like tuned in to one another musically. And by that, I mean the people in England — the Beatles people, the Stones people, the Kinks — and the Beach Boys, even though we were in a geographically different place," said Cavaliere. "We were all falling in love."

The cover for the *Groovin'* album — which shows the band members drawn in caricature —was conceived, but not illustrated, by drummer Danelli.

"I was pretty heavily into art in those days, so I kind of directed where we went with our graphics and things like that," said Danelli. "I didn't do the actual cartoon drawing on the cover. That was done by a friend of mine, Lynn Rubin. But we talked about the concept, what we wanted to do, which was take a comic book approach to it. That was kind of the style in those days. I used to love doing the whole trip of the packaging of an album. It was just a ton of fun."

The cover also featured a sticker on the front that read "This LP has the big hit" followed by either "How Can I Be Sure" or "A Girl Like You," both of which were Top 10 hits.

The Young Rascals would eventually change their name to the Rascals after the release of the *Groovin'* album. The band would experience more chart success with two more

Top 5 singles, "People Got to Be Free," which got to No. 1, and "A Beautiful Morning," which got to No. 3, both in 1968.

By 1970, Brigati had left the group, and Cornish followed in 1971. Because the band contractually owed Atlantic Records one more album, the seventh and final studio album, *Search and Nearness,* was released in 1971, but included tracks that were recorded in 1969 and 1970.

The Rascals were inducted into the Rock and Roll Hall of Fame in 1997. Steven Van Zandt, a member of Bruce Springsteen's E Street Band and a Rock and Roll Hall of Famer himself, delivered the induction speech for the Rascals. It was the first time in years that the four original members of the band — Brigati, Cavaliere, Cornish and Danelli — had appeared together on stage. They performed "Good Lovin'," "Groovin'," "How Can I Be Sure," and "People Got to Be Free" at the ceremony.

That appearance planted the seed of a reunion, which was encouraged by Van Zandt. But Van Zandt couldn't make it happen until 2012 when the Rascals reunited for the "Once Upon a Dream" reunion, which lasted for six performances at the Capitol Theatre in Port Chester, New York. The shows were produced and directed by Van Zandt and his wife, Maureen.

"Stevie had been trying to get the Rascals back together for thirty-five years. He's an avid Rascals fan," said Danelli. "He saw us when we were a really potent live act when we first started, and he never got over it."

Danelli wasn't convinced that Van Zandt could pull it off, given the internal creative differences within the band that caused it to split in 1970.

"But it was years and years ago and whatever hatchets were around were buried long ago," said Danelli. "Everybody had forgotten; there was no ill will. Everybody was positive and feeling good about still playing our music.

And it's evident in the show. Everybody is still really potent, everybody is strong."

But once again, it wouldn't last. The Rascals continued with 15 more performances of "Once Upon a Dream" in 2013, a combination concert and theatrical event, after which the band members once again went their separate ways.

The music of the Rascals, however, appears to transcend generations and continues to be popular.

"It's kind of a surprise to me, a blessing to me. I don't even know how to describe it. The only thing I can say is that the intent that was put into the music in those days, it really is still shining," said Cavaliere. "Those songs were about love. Most of the songs were joyous kind of events that happened in the studio and were captured on tape in those days. I guess that comes through the airwaves still. It's amazing, really.

"We were so young. I went to see Paul McCartney a couple years back and we were backstage and he said, 'Man, do you have any idea how young we all were?' We can't imagine our kids doing what we did, which was being part of the national, international music scene. It was incredible," he said.

Guitarist Gene Cornish and drummer Dino Danelli were happy with the *Groovin'* album when it was finished. And Danelli conceived the album cover, which shows the band members drawn in caricature.
(Photo by Mike Morsch)

Discography

The Young Rascals

"Groovin'"

Released July 31, 1967

All songs are written by Felix Cavaliere and Eddie Brigati, except where otherwise indicated.

Side One

1. A Girl Like You (2:51) - Lead Vocals: Felix
2. Find Somebody (3:48) - Lead Vocals: Eddie
3. I'm So Happy Now (Gene Cornish) (2:50) - Lead Vocals: Gene
4. Sueño (2:48) - Lead Vocals: Felix (also written by Cavaliere and Brigati but attributed incorrectly to another writer on some labels)[3]
5. How Can I Be Sure (2:56) - Lead Vocals: Eddie

Side Two

1. Groovin' (2:33) - Lead Vocals: Felix
2. If You Knew (3:04) - Lead Vocals: Eddie & Felix
3. I Don't Love You Anymore (Cornish) (3:09 - Lead Vocals: Gene
4. You Better Run (2:28)- Lead Vocals: Felix
5. A Place in the Sun (Ronald Miller, Brian Wells) (4:52) - Lead Vocals: Eddie
6. It's Love (3:15) - Lead Vocals - Felix

A rollercoaster ride that you wouldn't believe

Insight Out

The Association

(1967)

Ruthann Friedman was kind of like a den mother for Jules Alexander, Russ Giguere, Ted Bluechel, Jr., and Jim Yester.

The four artists, members of the band The Association, lived together in a house in Hollywood. Friedman was a friend who had been introduced to the guys by Van Dyke Parks, a lyricist who in early 1966 had collaborated with Brian Wilson on the Beach Boys' *Smile* Project.

Friedman wrote what some of The Association members thought were real outside-the-box songs. There was one stretch in the mid-1960s when she slept on the couch at the Hollywood house of The Association members for several weeks while trying to find a place to live.

The search for a place to call her own led Friedman from Hollywood up the California coast to San Francisco, where she bunked for a time at the home of David Crosby, then a member of the Byrds.

Tom Shipley was a songwriter who had sold a couple of songs to A&M Records and the record company thought he had potential. So they put Shipley together with Friedman and Tandyn Almer and called them The Garden Club. Almer had written the single "Along Comes Mary," which The Association had put on its 1966 debut album *And Then . . .*

Jim Yester, rhythm guitarist and vocalist for The Association, said the band finished recording the vocals for "Windy" around 4 a.m., just ahead of an 8 a.m. scheduled flight out of Los Angeles to Birmingham, Alabama, for a gig there. (Photo by Mike Morsch)

Along Comes the Association. The song was a hit that reached No. 7 on the U.S. Billboard Hot 100 Singles chart.

Friedman and Shipley continued to write songs once Friedman had moved into Crosby's basement. One evening, Friedman asked Shipley to come over. She was working on a song and wanted him to help her finish it.

But Shipley was also writing songs with another songwriter, Michael Brewer, and they were working on one that evening called "She Thinks She's a Woman."

"And I said, 'Ruthann, I'll tell you what — I'll make it tomorrow night,'" Shipley recalled telling Friedman. "So she finished the song by herself that night."

Shipley eventually helped Friedman cut the demo for the song. When Friedman returned to Hollywood several weeks later, she again approached The Association, this time with a completed song and demo in hand for the band's consideration.

Songwriter Tom Shipley was supposed to help fellow songwriter Ruthann Friedman finish the lyrics for the song "Windy," but instead spent the evening writing with Michael Brewer leaving Friedman to finish the song by herself in the basement of David Crosby's house.
(Photo by Mike Morsch)

"She came back from San Francisco and said, 'When I was out there, I wrote this kind of contemporary song. But I don't know if it's too folksy for you guys,'" recalled Jim Yester, rhythm guitarist and vocalist for The Association. "She sat down on the kitchen floor with her guitar and played us the song. We thought, oh, that's kind of neat."

The song was "Windy."

In just five months in 1966, from July to November, The Association had released its first two albums, *And Then . . . Along Comes the Association* and *Renaissan ce* for Valiant Records. The first album featured two hit singles, "Along Comes Mary," and "Cherish," which was the band's first No. 1 song on the Hot 100 Singles chart.

The band had already started working on some songs for its next album, which would be called *Insight Out,* most notably "Never My Love" and "Requiem for the Masses," when Valiant went out of business and was absorbed by its distributor, Warner Brothers. The band's first album was produced by Curt Boettcher and the second album was produced by Jim Yester's brother, Jerry Yester, who had handled the production of the first two songs.

The switch to Warner Brothers coincided with The Association's desire to elevate the band from the regional music scene to the national level. Bones Howe, a well-known recording engineer who had recorded "California Dreamin'" and "Monday, Monday" for The Mamas & The Papas, was chosen to produce The Association's *Insight Out* album — and Jerry Yester was out.

Michael Brewer was asked to join The Association, but declined the opportunity because he was writing songs with Tom Shipley at the time. Brewer and Shipley would go on to write and record the No. 1 single, "One Toke Over the Line." (Photo by Mike Morsch)

When The Association heard Friedman's "Windy," they wanted Howe to hear it.

"So we had Ruth play it for Bones and he said, 'I got an idea for that.' Bones had an idea that if we stuck to the folk idiom, with a driving rock background — kind of the way that 'Windy' is — that we would have that tag forever."

Another part of the Warner deal for *Insight Out* was that in addition to having Howe produce, he was also going to use the best studio musicians in Los Angeles, known as The Wrecking Crew, who had just completed recording *Pet Sounds* for Brian Wilson and the Beach Boys.

According to Jim Yester, the band had finished a recording that included the vocals for "Windy" around 4 a.m., just ahead of an 8 a.m. scheduled flight out of Los Angeles to Birmingham, Alabama, for a gig there.

During the recording sessions for the album, Jules Alexander decided to leave the band. He wasn't in on the recording session for "Windy," but he was honoring some of the concert commitments the band had already made, so he was on the plane to Birmingham, along with a tape of the "Windy" recording session.

"Once we got to the auditorium in Birmingham, we put that tape on the sound system and played it and we all went totally bananas," said Yester. "We were dancing around the auditorium and we thought, man, that is a smash. And it was. It went up the charts so fast it made our heads spin.

"We had no idea at the time who The Wrecking Crew was, even though on our first album, a lot of the early Wrecking Crew guys were involved [guitarist Mike Deasy, bassist Jerry Scheff and percussionists Jim Troxel and Toxey French]," said Yester. "They turned out to be fantastic. They were such incredible guys, not only monster musicians, but just the neatest guys. Any ideas that you had, they immediately snapped right on them."

In between concert gigs, The Association continued to record the songs for *Insight Out*. But now it was faced with finding a replacement for Alexander.

The band members interviewed Michael Brewer, whom they knew from Los Angeles, but they didn't hire him.

"Terry Kirkman was a friend of mine and he used to come by all the time," said Brewer. "He would say, 'Would you like to join The Association?' This was about the time Tom [Shipley] and I were really writing songs and going into the studio and enjoying our songs. I thought I could join a group with a bunch of guys and once in a while maybe get to do a song of mine. Or I could have a partner and we could do

Guitarist and vocalist Jules Alexander decided to leave The Association during the recording of the *Insight Out* album, but stayed on to fulfill some concert commitments for the band.
(Photo bv Mike Morsch)

all of our own songs. And I have absolutely no regrets. I made the right choice."

Brewer and Shipley would go on a few years later to form a duo and record the hit single "One Toke Over the Line."

But The Association was still seeking a replacement for Alexander.

During one of the group's recording sessions for *Insight Out,* Larry Ramos, a one-time member of the New Christy Minstrels who had embarked on a solo career, was recording with a friend the same day in an adjacent studio.

Terry Kirkman, who played wind instruments, provided vocals for The Association, and had written "Cherish" for the band, approached Ramos and asked him to join the group.

Ramos said yes.

"When I joined the group, I noticed that the guys were very careful about the music that they selected," said Ramos. "They had done two albums and they had two hits. From hundreds and hundreds of pieces of music that were submitted to us — and we also wrote our own music — we didn't care about where the music came from as long as it was good. If we were fortunate to have written the music and it was good enough, then more power to the guys who wrote it."

"Never My Love" was one of the songs that the band had selected to record before Ramos joined the group. The Addrisi Brothers, Don and Dick, had written the song, and it was one that the brothers had played for The Association at the Hollywood house.

"It's a classic. I love that song and I loved it the first time I ever heard it," said Ramos. "There are certain things that you look for in a piece of music when you record it — the memorable melodies, the memorable lyrics – that has a lot to do with it. And the production of the recording itself. You have to have all of those elements together to have a successful record. And we were very, very fortunate that we had all of these happening to us not just once, not just twice, not just three times, but several times. It surprised many of the guys in the group that we were fortunate to have all these hits."

Touring between recording sessions for *Insight Out* still presented a challenge for the band, even after Ramos joined. Alexander was still committed to the touring schedule, although not the recording sessions. So Ramos initially went on tour with the band, but just to watch.

There was an incident on the road, though, that forced Ramos into the touring band. One afternoon before a concert, the guys were driving around and bassist Brian Cole was throwing firecrackers out of the car window. But Cole hung onto one of the firecrackers too long and it blew up in his hand. The result was that he couldn't play bass for that evening's show.

"So that night we said, 'OK, Larry, here is your baptism by fire.' Jules went to bass and Larry went to lead guitar," said Yester.

Ramos was now a full-fledged member of the studio group recording *Insight Out* and the touring band.

In addition to The Wrecking Crew, the *Insight Out* recording sessions also included the band working with vocal arranger Clark Burroughs, who was a tenor for a group called the Hi-Lo's.

"Clark did phenomenal work. We would have three mics in a semicircle and he would sit on the inside of the semicircle on a stool and direct us. He had headphones on so he could hear everything. And he'd move guys back and move guys up, have guys sing louder. It was just fantastic," said Yester.

"The arrangement that you hear on the record, the vocal harmonies, are really kind of suppressed. Bones liked to mix it where you got the feel of the background voices but you couldn't really hear the actual parts, except in the places where it was a third and a fifth. We would sing the harmonies and then we'd add parts. It was just incredible-sounding," he said.

Released ahead of the album, the single "Windy" would become the band's next No. 1 single on the U.S. Billboard Hot 100 Singles chart. The follow-up single, "Never My Love," also released in advance of the album and recorded before "Windy," reached No. 2 on the U.S. Billboard Hot 100 Singles.

The two songs would go on to be among the most-played singles of the late 1960s, and virtually assured the success of the *Insight Out* album. It would peak at No. 8 on the U.S. Billboard Top LPs chart and become one of the top-selling albums of 1967.

"We pretty well knew upfront — because of the release of the two singles — that the album was going to do well, which turned out to be the case. If you have one hit on an album, that's great. Two hits on an album, that's fantastic," said Yester.

The timing of the album's release, in June 1967, also turned out to be fortuitous for the band. That same month, from June 16 to 18, the Monterey International Pop Music Festival was held at the Monterey County Fairgrounds in Monterey, California. And The Association was asked to be the opening act for the three-day festival.

Producer Howe's relationship with Lou Adler, who had produced The Mamas & The Papas, and the fact that The Association had opened for The Mamas & The Papas, secured the Monterey gig for The Association.

"That was an incredible trip. Lou Adler threw us onstage and the cameras weren't set up and the sound system wasn't ready to go. There were two sets of drums on stage, Hal Blaine [drummer for The Wrecking Crew] had set up and our drummer, Ted Bluechel, set up on what he thought were his drums. When we got up onstage, Ted realized he wasn't on his drums and needed about five minutes to get set up. And the announcement came, 'Here they are, The Association!' and we were just all standing there," said Yester.

The introduction of the band to the Monterey crowd was made by John Phillips of The Mamas & The Papas.

"We opened with 'Enter the Young' and the cameras didn't even get that. Fortunately, they got 'Along Comes Mary' [the second song in the set]. It was so incredible to open that show, and then for the rest of the three days, have seats about twelve feet away from the front of the stage," said Yester.

"Windy" was the third song in The Association's Monterey set list, but the rest of the songs in the set have apparently been lost to history.

"I don't think we played 'Never My Love' at Monterey. I don't think it was included in our set at the time," said Yester.

"I don't think we ever fit into the scene at any time. When we first came out, what was going on was some pretty heavy acid stuff. We were all these ex-folkies and we were doing love ballads. But we were also doing some stuff that was heavier. 'Along Comes Mary,' I wouldn't really call a folk song or a love song," said Yester. "According to Tandyn Almer, who wrote it, it's about a social protest. Protesting the fact that everybody was putting pot down and yet pills and alcohol were legal. It wasn't saying hey, let's all go smoke pot; it was saying let's have a level playing field."

As for the making of *Insight Out,* Yester called it "a roller coaster ride that you wouldn't believe."

"It's one of the best for sure," he said. "It was pretty much a Bones Howe production of The Association. Bones did a magnificent job. What he did was incredible and I'll always be thankful to him for that. He had marvelous ideas and was great to work with."

Discography

The Association
"Insight Out"
Released June 1967

Side one
1. Wasn't It a Bit Like Now? (3:33) Terry Kirkman
2. On a Quiet Night (3:21(P. F. Sloan
3. We Love Us (2:25) Ted Bluechel
4. When Love Comes to Me (2:45) Jim Yester
5. Windy (2:56) Ruthann Friedman
6. Reputation (2:38) Tim Hardin

Side two
1. Never My Love (3:10) Don Addrisi, Dick Addrisi
2. Happiness Is (2:13) Don Addrisi, Dick Addrisi
3. Sometime (2:38) Russ Giguere
4. Wantin' Ain't Gettin' (2:20) Mike Deasy
5. Requiem for the Masses (4:06) Terry Kirkman

A Civil War buff disc jockey was the difference-maker

WOMAN, WOMAN

Gary Puckett and the Union Gap

(1968)

As he was sitting in Studio A getting ready to cut a song for Columbia Records, Gary Puckett looked at what was going on around him.

Studio A was one of four main recording studios at Columbia, in the CBS building on Sunset Boulevard in Hollywood, California. And it was the biggest recording room in the building.

Producer and songwriter Jerry Fuller, tasked by Columbia with finding talent and developing hit songs for artists, had signed Gary Puckett and the Union Gap. And Fuller had a song he was certain was going to be a hit for the band.

In addition to the members of the Union Gap — Kerry Chater on bass, Gary "Mutha" Withem on keyboards, Dwight Bement on tenor sax and Paul Wheatbread on drums — Fuller had hired an entire orchestra of around 30 pieces to play on the record. As Puckett looked around the studio, he saw Glen Campbell on guitar, Carol Kaye on bass, Larry Knechtel on piano and Hal Blaine behind the drum set.

Gary Puckett was so overcome with emotion at listening to the Wrecking Crew record the music for "Woman, Woman" that he had to stop singing the lead vocals in the studio and just listen to the beautiful music. (Photo by Mike Morsch)

It was The Wrecking Crew, a nickname bestowed by Blaine on the group of studio musicians who played — oftentimes anonymously in those days — on many of the most successful albums of the 1960s. By that point, The Wrecking Crew had worked with Jan and Dean, the Righteous Brothers, the Beach Boys, the Byrds, The Association, The Mamas & The Papas, Sonny & Cher, Simon & Garfunkel, and Frank Sinatra.

The Wrecking Crew were the very best in the business. The Union Gap members, with the exception of Wheatbread, were among the musicians playing on the record, but all the heavy musical lifting was done by The Wrecking Crew.

It was the fall of 1967 and it was the first time that Gary Puckett and the Union Gap had been in a big-league recording session of that kind.

"It was an exciting day for me because I had never done anything to that extent. Yes, I had been in the studio and yes, we had tried to make records prior to that. And we actually made a couple of good efforts, but we knew nothing of producing. We had to kind of learn that stuff as we went along.

"But I'm looking at the engineer and I'm looking at the producer and I'm looking at the setup in the studio and here we are with the big monitors. It was beautiful," said Puckett.

And then the musicians started to play.

"I was supposed to sing live. But I was so overcome with the emotion of it all that it just nearly made me cry. Jerry, being the great producer that he was, and the engineer, being the great engineer that he was — it already sounded so incredible to me that I just said, 'Guys, excuse me but I'm going to just sit back and listen because I really can't contain this emotion,'" said Puckett.

"So the tracks were done without me singing, but with me sitting there with those headphones on and just going, 'My gosh, I get to be the focal point of this whole collage of beautiful music.'"

The song they were recording that day, "Woman, Woman," which would go on to hit No. 3 on the Cash Box chart and No. 4 on the Billboard Hot 100 Singles chart in early 1968, eventually anchored the first studio album of the same name by Gary Puckett and the Union Gap for Columbia Records.

Although The Wrecking Crew would be hired to play on all the songs on the *Woman, Woman* album, Puckett and the Union Gap would record only three songs in those first few sessions: the title track, written by Jim Glaser and Jimmy Payne; "Don't Make Promises," written by Tim Hardin; and "Believe Me," written by Puckett.

"Woman, Woman" was the first single released on September 16, 1967, and appeared on the A-side of the record, with "Don't Make Promises" on the B-side. The Columbia distribution staff liked what it heard on the record, which meant that it would be aggressively promoted to radio stations.

Stations usually had programs and disc jockeys that could make or break a record with extended play — or not — in their regular rotations.

But from the get-go, the record was getting "split" airtime, which meant some markets liked "Woman, Woman" while others would flip the record over and play "Don't Make Promises." As a result, neither single could sustain traction in any market across the United States.

"I remember Jerry saying to me at some point, 'You know, I think we're going to have to go back in [to the studio] and try again because we can't seem to find a market that is strong enough with either side to make it a hit record,'" said Puckett.

Amidst the plethora of records being recorded and pushed out to radio stations, Puckett believed theirs needed a little extra something to set it apart from the others. Fortunately, he had an idea that would prove to be exactly what the record needed.

From the beginning, he thought the band should have a different look. It was a time when fashion was dominated by tie-dyed colors, leather with fringes, holes in the knees of blue jeans, and platform shoes. Not only was everybody on the street wearing pretty much the same thing, so was everybody on stage.

"I had come up with this idea that we would look different and the way we would do it was to wear Union soldier outfits from the Civil War period in time," said Puckett. "And as it turns out, I had to fight with the record company. And they finally relented."

When the "Woman, Woman" single was released, there was an authentic-looking sepia-tone picture of the group on the front cover. The photo also took on a Civil War period "look" because it was taken in front of a pile of rubble in the Van Nuys neighborhood of Los Angeles.

The photo got the attention of the program director at a radio station in Columbus, Ohio, who just happened to be a Civil War buff. He liked it so much that it made him wonder what the record sounded like. He played it, loved it, and put it in the station's regular play rotation, where it soon went to No. 1 in the Columbus market.

Columbia Records now had a foothold with a popular record in a major market and it wanted to expand that market outside of Columbus. Company officials contacted the band members in San Diego, where they all lived at the time, and told them to pack their bags. They were going to be playing gigs in nearby Cleveland to help support the record.

But winter was just starting to grip Cleveland in late 1967.

Every day, Puckett, along with Columbia sales representative Steve Popovich — who in 1972 would be named the first-ever vice president of promotions for Columbia Records — would go to all the radio stations in the Cleveland market, introduce themselves to program directors, and give them the "Woman, Woman" record.

Then every evening, the band would play gigs at a place called Otto's Grotto, which was in the basement of a Sheraton Hotel in Cleveland.

"You know, Cleveland in the winter is no day at the beach, that's for sure," said Puckett.

Once "Woman, Woman" became a hit single, Columbia decided to invest more money to finish the band's debut album of the same name. So Puckett and the Union Gap — along with The Wrecking Crew — went back into the studio.

Producer Fuller started pulling the rest of the album together and getting arrangements done for the songs. Fuller and Columbia were in charge of all aspects of the album.

A big part of preparing the group for fame was that the "machine" wasn't yet in place to get Gary Puckett and the

Union Gap fully out into the marketplace. The Williams Morris Agency was hired to work with the band.

Fuller also chose the rest of the songs to fill out the album. And he chose songs that he had calculated to be a sure bet: "By the Time I Get to Phoenix," written by Jimmy Webb and recorded by Glen Campbell (the same Glen Campbell who, despite the success of the song, had yet to be able to leave his steady gig as a session guitarist with The Wrecking Crew and pursue a solo career); "Kentucky Woman" by Neil Diamond; "You Better Sit Down Kids," written by Sonny Bono; and "To Love Somebody," written by Barry Gibb and Robin Gibb of the Bee Gees.

All those songs had been released in 1967 and all had proven to be successful for those artists.

"It was Jerry's boat and he was sailing it. And his philosophy was that these were all great songs, these were all popular songs, millions of people love these songs, millions of people are going to love your song, and they're probably going to be very happy to hear you sing some of these other songs," said Puckett.

The songwriting contributions by the band members on the album included Puckett's "Believe Me"; "I Want a New Day" written by Chater; and "My Son," written by Chater and Withem.

The *Woman, Woman* album would be released in January 1968. The title track would hit No. 3 on the Cash Box Top 100 chart, and No. 4 on the Billboard Hot 100 Singles chart. The album itself would reach No. 22 on the Billboard Hot 200 Albums chart.

The album cover, showing the band members wearing their Civil War uniforms, was taken in a rural area about an hour from New York City. The photo included the band members holding muskets and featured some smoke bombs that had been deployed to give the photo a more authentic look.

Although the formula for the first album would carry on through the next two albums, *Young Girl* and *Union Gap*, both also released in 1968, the band members themselves didn't really like the song "Woman, Woman."

And the reason was simple: The band had expected to play a bigger role in the recording, something more of a band-oriented, five-man thing. What they got was overshadowed by The Wrecking Crew.

"What we ended up with was a singer with an orchestra. The band became sort of superfluous in a way. You couldn't pick them out in the background. They were a part of thirty pieces. They were disappointed in that regard," said Puckett.

"I was not disappointed. I thought we were making a really great record. But as far as the sense of making a hit record, Jerry was going 'Yeah man, this is great. This is terrific.' He was very enthusiastic about it because he loved the song," he said.

"Jerry loved my voice, he loved the idea of the outfits, that kind of stuff. His charge was to stay within budget and make records that Columbia Records could make money on. And Jerry was very pleased," said Puckett. "I had that sense that he was happy. And I was hopeful, but I was certainly not certain that we had a hit record."

By the band's fourth album, *Incredible*, released in late 1968, Puckett and the rest of the band members wanted to write and produce their own work. In early 1969, Fuller had put together a 40-piece orchestra to record a song he had written for the band, but Puckett and the band members balked. They refused to participate in the recording session and it was canceled. Gary Puckett and the Union Gap never again worked with Jerry Fuller.

By 1970, Puckett began working as a solo act with the Union Gap as his backing band for live shows. By 1972, Puckett and his bandmates had parted.

To this day, though, Puckett still sings those songs that he and the Union Gap made famous in the late 1960s.

"People say to me 'Do you still love to sing those songs?' It's really kind of an odd question to me, although it's certainly not odd to those questioning," said Puckett. "But because the people love these songs so much and have the memories of these songs so deeply in their minds and hearts, they know the words, they know the melody to the string part and the horn part. They can sing along with you when the horns go up. They have it so ingrained in their souls that to watch them smile and sing along, I've got to love those songs, because the songs have treated me so well in that regard."

Discography

Gary Pucket and the Union Gap
"Woman, Woman"

Released Jan. 10, 1968

1. Woman, Woman. Jim Glaser, Jimmy Payne
2. M'Lady. Steve Karliski
3. By the Time I Get to Phoenix ( ) Jimmy Webb
4. Paindrops. Jerry Fuller
5. Believe Me. Gary Puckett
6. I Want a New Day. Kerry Chater
7. You Better Sit Down Kids. Sonny Bono
8. Kentucky Woman. Neil Diamond
9 My Son (version 1). Gary Withem, Kerry Chater
10. To Love Somebody. Barry Gibb, Robin Gibb
11. Don't Make Promises. Tim Hardin

Simon says, bubblegum pop deserved more respect

SIMON SAYS
1910 Fruitgum Company
(1968)

During the summer of 1967, music producer Jeff Katz had gone to a swim club to hear a band he hoped to sign to a record deal. He had gotten his hands on an acetate that the group had cut that contained four original songs, and Katz liked what he heard.

Katz and Jerry Kasenetz were partners in a recording production company called Super K Productions, under the auspices of Buddha Records. Negotiations between Katz and the band went back and forth for a few months, but by October 1967, the group had signed with Super K Productions/Buddha Records.

"Probably a month later, in November, Katz said, 'I've got this song I want you to record.' And he played it for us," said Frank Jeckell, whose band Jeckell and the Hydes had formed in New Jersey in 1966, and whose members would form the nucleus of the new band. "We said, 'Well, that's nice, but it wasn't what our deal was. We were going to record our original material and move forward with that. That's what you agreed to, right?'"

Katz brushed off the concern.

"He goes, 'Yeah, yeah, yeah, but I think this is a hit. Can you guys take it and see what you can do with it?'" said Jeckell. "We had a little powwow, and the unanimous decision was that this song was a piece of crap, we want nothing to do with it, and we're not gonna touch it."

At the time, the band members were mostly teenagers, with Jeckell being the oldest at 21 years old. The others included Mark Gutkowski, Floyd Marcus, Pat Karwan and Steve Mortkowitz, all from Linden, New Jersey.

As the oldest band member, though, Jeckell was the de facto voice of reason within the group.

"I said, listen, yeah, you're right, this is crap," said Jeckell. "We don't want to play this kind of music. It's stupid and it's dumb. But if this is what they want us to do, what the hell, let's just see what we can do with it and get it over with," said Jeckell.

So the band put together its version and it didn't sound any better than the original demo tape that Katz had given to them.

"It was still a piece of crap and it wasn't going to go anywhere," said Jeckell.

But then Jeckell had an idea: Why not give the song a "Wooly Bully" feel?

"Wooly Bully" was a single from an album of the same name by Sam the Sham and the Pharaohs, which had sold three million copies and reached No. 2 on the U.S. Billboard Hot 100 Singles chart in June 1965.

So that's what the band did. It gave a "Wooly Bully" feel to the song that Katz was certain was going to be a hit. And then the band members took it to Katz for a listen.

"Jeff jumped out of his chair and yelled, 'That's it!' And in December, we recorded it," said Jeckell.

As it turned out, Katz was right. By January 1968, the single "Simon Says," by his new band the 1910 Fruitgum Company, went to No. 4 on the U.S. Billboard Hot 100 Singles chart, and got as high as No. 2 on the charts in both the United Kingdom and Australia.

Frank Jeckell of the 1910 Fuitgum Company said he and the band didn't want to record the song "Simon Says" as it was presented, so they decided to give it a "Wooly Bully" treatment.
(Photo by Mike Morsch)

Not only that, but the song is arguably the inspiration for what was to be known as the "bubblegum pop" genre of music.

Now, the 1910 Fruitgum Company had a hit single and it needed to make an album while the song was hot and the public's interest was piqued.

Acording to Jeckell, the album, which would also be titled *Simon Says,* faced some hurdles from the get-go. And the biggest hurdle was that the producers, Katz and Kasenetz, made it clear they wanted the track selection of the album to mirror the kind of "material" that was similar to the voice of the "Simon Says" single.

Fortunately, according to Jeckell, he had written a song called "Magic Windmill," and Marcus, who was a prolific songwriter, had three songs — "Keep Your Thoughts on the Bright Side," "The Year 2001" and "Bubblegum World" — that the band believed would work on the album. Karwan contributed "The Story of Flipper," and Elliot Chiprut, who had written "Simon Says," had three more songs that the band chose: "Pop Goes the Weasel," "May I Take a Giant Step (Into Your Heart)," and "Happy Little Teardrops."

The album would be rounded out by "(Poor Old) Mr. Jensen," written by Katz, Kasenetz, and David Taxin; and "Soul Struttin'," that was co-written by eventual 1970s recording star Tony Orlando.

"We didn't really get an opportunity to pick the style of the material that we wanted the direction of the group to go in. But on the other hand, we didn't think what we created was garbage either, because it was creative and the songs are good songs for the most part. We felt that we did a good job at putting them on the record," said Jeckell.

"If anything on the album was a throwaway, it was the song by Tony Orlando. And it was put there because we wanted to give Steve [Mortkowitz] — who was one of the best harmony singers but probably the weakest lead vocalist — a chance to do something. If you listen to that song carefully, you can hear that he's not a lead vocalist. But we wanted to give him an option to participate on a lead level on at least one song. That's where that came from," said Jeckell.

With a hit single, things changed for the band. It got the band what Jeckell called "massive recognition" across the country, and a trip to California to appear on *American Bandstand* with Dick Clark. It also got the group an invitation to be on *The Ed Sullivan Show*, but that appearance got preempted by the assassination of Senator Robert F. Kennedy on June 6, 1968. The *Sullivan* show appearance was never rescheduled.

But the band also got something that it didn't anticipate: scorn, particularly from within the music industry.

"You would think that with all of that, we would have been on top of the world. And to a tiny degree — and I use the word 'tiny' purposely — we were," said Jeckell. "But other things came into play that made the experience not so much fun for us. The biggest factor was either the lack of, or seriously negative, response we got from our peers in the business. They thought we were a joke. They thought we were not to be respected, not to be highly regarded in any way, shape, or form. Not even to be talked to in most cases."

The fact that the band members had a negative rapport with their peers weighed heavily on their young minds, according to Jeckell, who opted for a more pragmatic approach.

"I didn't like it, but I was perfectly happy rolling along and putting out hits," said Jeckell. "As I told the other guys at the time, listen, all right, this sucks that people are dissing us. But stay with it, keep with it, and when we get more hits going and our names become more recognizable, we can break out of this stranglehold we're in and start doing our own stuff and change direction. Just relax; let it grow into something."

But some of the and members didn't agree with that approach. By mid-1968, just weeks after the release of the *Simon Says* album in April, drummer Marcus decided to leave the band. He was quickly followed out the door a few weeks later by bassist Mortkowitz. In late August 1968, guitarist Karwan was gone, leaving only Jeckell and Gutkowski as original members by September 1968.

In addition to the lack of respect from their peers, the band members hadn't been paid any royalties from the hit single "Simon Says." The original members — with the exception of Gutkowski — hired a lawyer and served Super K Productions with papers in September 1968 suing the company for nonpayment of royalties.

"And that's when they [the company] invited me to leave the band," said Jeckell. "I was kind of surprised, but I should have known they would do that. They had a contract that would allow them to do that. They owned the name, so they could do whatever they wanted. We were just hired hands on the contracts. And that was that."

Because success came quickly for the 1910 Fruitgum Company — and appeared to end just as quickly — there have been conflicting reports over the years about whether the original band members played on their albums at all or if session musicians were used.

According to Jeckell, the five original members were the only players on both the *Simon Says* album and the band's next album, *1, 2, 3 Red Light,* which was released in October 1968, after the original members had split up.

But according to Jeckell, there is a distinction.

"Jeff Katz knew that we were a crackerjack recording team because we had put out a quality album, a quality piece of work with the *Simon Says* album," said Jeckell. "So we called Steve and Floyd back and the original five guys went into the studio and we knocked off the *1, 2, 3 Red Light* album. But we didn't play on the single '1, 2, 3 Red Light' because we were touring when that was cut by the studio band. But the album, except for '1, 2, 3 Red Light,' was all us."

The single "1, 2, 3 Red Light," written by Sal Trimachi and Bobby Trimachi, would become the band's next hit, peaking at No. 5 on the U.S. Billboard Hot 100 Singles chart and No. 3 on the U.S. Cash Box Top 100 Singles chart.

"I was in the office with Jeff [Katz] when Sal Trimachi came in with his beat-up old guitar case to sell this song he wrote. Sal was ragged with torn-up jeans and long, straggly, unwashed, unkempt hair. He looked like a bum, like a very old man who was barely getting by. I think he might have been forty," said Jeckell. "But he opened up the case, got out the guitar and played '1, 2, 3 Red Light' for Jeff. I had no particular feeling at the time that it was a hit. But I knew that it certainly fit in with the bubblegum pop direction that both the 1910 Fruitgum Company and the Ohio Express were being taken in. So I knew it would be a good fit there, but I didn't know it was going to be a hit."

And therein lies another band — the Ohio Express — that often gets mistaken for the 1910 Fruitgum Company. Part of the reason is that the Ohio Express was also in the Super K Productions stable of artists and the band was also producing bubblegum pop hits like "Yummy, Yummy, Yummy," which was released in April 1968, the same timeframe in which the 1910 Fruitgum Company was experiencing its increased popularity.

Joey Levine was the co-writer and sang lead on "Yummy, Yummy, Yummy" for the Ohio Express.

"Joey Levine never appeared on any Fruitgum records, never wrote a Fruitgum record, was never even in the studio when a Fruitgum record was recorded," said Jeckell. "So I hate — really, really hate with a passion — this garbage misinformation that I have to keep refuting over and over and over again because people seem to find it and always manage to ask me, 'Were you really a band?' My response is, go fuck yourself. That's what I want to say."

But after five decades, Jeckell understands the confusion that surrounds the 1910 Fruitgum Company and the Ohio Express and whether they were "real" bands or just fictional entities or bands with interchangeable parts that Super K Productions used to churn out hits in the late 1960s.

"When people meet us for the first time and hear the name, they say, 'Oh yeah, right, "Yummy, Yummy, Yummy."' That's the response we get. And for a while, we would just correct people and say, 'No, that was the Ohio Express'" said Jeckell. "But then there is a reality here. If you look on the *1, 2, 3 Red Light* album, you will hear the Ohio Express track, which, by the way, wasn't recorded by the Ohio Express, it was recorded by the studio musicians, for 'Yummy, Yummy, Yummy,' with our lead vocalist, Mark, singing it. So the fact is, there is a bona fide real version of 'Yummy, Yummy, Yummy' by the 1910 Fruitgum Company. It wasn't the one that was the hit record, but it does exist. So we stopped correcting people and we even include the song in our show. People want to think that, fine, we'll take it."

As for bubblegum pop, Jeckell believes that the 1910 Fruitgum Company was one of the primary progenitors of, and is in some respects the creator of, the genre.

"I have no way to verify or validate this, but one of Floyd's songs that was on the first album was called 'Bubblegum World.' We think there is a good possibility that the term bubblegum pop came about because that song was on the album with that title," he said.

And Jeckell said that anyone who wants to know what kind of music the 1910 Fruitgum Company really wanted to play can just flip over the single "Simon Says" and listen to the B-side.

As a reward for not making a big fuss over recording the "Simon Says" single, Katz told the band members that they could choose what song would go on the B-side. And they chose a song called "Reflections from the Looking Glass," written by keyboardist Gutkowski, the first song he had ever written. All the band members liked it.

"So we recorded it and Jeff listened to it and said, 'We're not going to put this out. The lyrics are too suggestive.' So I said OK. I went back and modified several spots in the lyrics to tone down what he was objecting to," said Jeckell. "If you listen to that song, though, it does show a good example, maybe the only example, of the kind of style we were looking to go into.

"Right then in 1967, the Beatles were in the studio working on *Sgt. Pepper*. We felt that we were contemporary and we were playing psychedelic-themed material. And that was where we were going. We were going to become another Strawberry Alarm Clock or something like that, playing that kind of music. That's where we wanted to be, that's what we thought was the cool thing to do at the time and we felt that we had the ammunition. We thought we had the vocals, we thought we had the instrumentation as well as the ability to write material and be successful at that. And I think given a chance, we may very well have," said Jeckell.

As for how the band got its name, the liner notes inside the original album state: "It was Frank, while going through an old trunk in the attic and finding an old bubblegum wrapper, who thought up the name 1910 Fruitgum Company."

"That's the mythology, which I kind of like in a way. It's mysterious and anybody who comes across it thinks that's cool," said Jeckell. "Because the truth is boring."

The band had one more gold record, a single called "Indian Giver" off a 1969 album by the same name. The song made it to No. 5 on the U.S. Billboard Hot 100 Singles chart. The only original member to appear on that album was Gutkowski.

As of 2017, Jeckell is the only original member performing under the band name 1910 Fruitgum Company.

Still, the music lives on, 50 years later.

"Despite the fact that it was bubblegum pop and bubblegum pop gets a bad rap for whatever reason, it's still good-time, happy-go-lucky, positive music which came about at a time in our country when we needed it," said Jeckell. "Things were bad with the Vietnam War, with all the demonstrations going on, then the race riots. It was not a good time, and anything that could be happy-go-lucky and take your mind off of it, even for a minute, was not a bad thing. I think the music played a huge role there and I'm glad to have been part of it."

Discography

1910 Fruitgum Company

"Simon Says"

Released April 1968

1. **Pop Goes the Weasel (1:58) Elliot Chiprut**
2. **Keep Your Thoughts on the Bright Side (2:20) Floyd Marcus**
3. **Magic Windmill (2:19) Frank Jeckell**
4. **The Year 2001 (1:51) Floyd Marcus**
5. **Soul Struttin' (2:38) Tony Orlando, Marty Thau**
6. **Simon Says (2:14) Elliot Chiprut**
7. **May I Take a Giant Step (Into Your Heart) (2:24) Elliot Chiprut**
8. **Bubblegum World (2:19) Floyd Marcus**
9. **Happy Little Teardrops (2:15) Elliot Chiprut**
10. **The Story of Flipper (4:30) Pat Karwan**
11. **(Poor Old) Mr. Jensen (2:15) Jerry Kasenetz, Jeff Katz, David Taxin**

A lost wallet in a New York cab leads to a megahit

AGE OF AQUARIUS

The 5th Dimension

(1969)

While out shopping in New York, Billy Davis, Jr. had lost his wallet in a cab. But he didn't know it.

It was 1968, and Davis and the other members of the 5th Dimension — Marilyn McCoo, Florence LaRue, Lamonte McLemore and Ron Townson — were riding a wave of popularity after the release of the group's third album, *Stoned Soul Picnic,* the title track of which had become a No. 3 hit single on the U.S. Billboard Hot 100 chart and a No. 2 hit single on the Hot R&B/Hip-Hop Songs chart.

The 5th Dimension was scheduled to perform at the Americana Hotel, just off Times Square. At that same time in 1968, the musical *Hair* was taking Broadway by storm. It was the hottest ticket on Broadway, and the members of the 5th Dimension wanted to see the show while they were in town. But there were no tickets to be had.

"We had been trying for the longest time to get in and see *Hair,* but nobody could get in because it was always sold out," said Davis. "Everybody wanted to see the show because everybody got naked in it. It was a big thing. That was a first onstage."

So Davis had instead decided to do some shopping that day ahead of the 5th Dimension performance scheduled for that evening at the Americana Hotel.

But when he exited the cab, Davis's wallet didn't go with him. The next customer in the cab found the wallet, checked for identification, and recognized whose wallet it was.

The man went inside the Americana, tracked down Davis, and returned the wallet. To show his appreciation, Davis gave the man tickets to that evening's performance by the 5th Dimension.

After the show that night, members of the 5th Dimension met up with the man. He had enjoyed the group's performance so much that he offered the group members tickets to *his* show.

"I had no idea he had a show," said Davis. "We come to find out that his name was Ed Gifford, and he was one of the producers of *Hair.* It was sold out, but Ed got us seats."

As it turned out, the tickets were all single seats. Although they weren't sitting together, the 5th Dimension members all attended the next day's performance of *Hair.*

It was during that performance that singer-actor Ronnie Dyson sang the song "Aquarius." And that song would take the 5th Dimension to even greater heights.

"We all gathered in the hall during intermission and said, 'We must do that song,'" said Davis.

They called their producer, Bones Howe, the next day and suggested to him that the 5th Dimension record "Aquarius." But Howe, who had produced the group's *Stoned Soul Picnic* album, was lukewarm on the idea. The song had been recorded and released by other artists without success.

"We had no knowledge of the history of the song, which was that it had already been recorded and released by a couple of other artists," said McCoo. "We just felt it would be a hit for us."

A few weeks later Howe called the group members with an idea: He wanted to take another song from *Hair* called "Let the Sunshine In" — referred to as "The Flesh Failures" — and tack it on the end of "Aquarius."

And that's what the 5th Dimension did. The group's next album, released in May 1969 on the Soul City label and called *Age of Aquarius,* was anchored by the title track, a medley called "Aquarius/Let the Sunshine In." It became the 5th Dimension's most successful album, reaching No. 2 on both the U.S. Billboard 200 Albums and R&B charts.

All because Davis had lost his wallet in a New York cab.

In the book *By the Time We Got to Woodstock: The Great Rock 'n' Roll Revolution of 1969,* by Bruce Pollock, Howe said that he had been bothered by the fact that there had been other releases of "Aquarius" and that none of them had done anything. So he eventually went to see *Hair* himself on Broadway.

"I was concerned about what we would do that would be any different," Howe told Pollock. "I went to see the show and there's a place where they do 'The Flesh Failures,' and at the end of the song is just a three-bar repeated thing of 'Let the sunshine in' where Ragni [Gerome Ragni, co-author of *Hair* and one of its stars in the Broadway production] was swinging across the stage on a chandelier and there was all kinds of craziness going on. That really stayed with me and I came out of the theater saying, I wonder if I could stick that on the end of 'Aquarius' and make that the ending."

Howe went back to his hotel and called Ragni, who along with James Rado and Galt MacDermot, had written the song.

"I mean, you don't mess with the music from a Broadway show. I started my professional career in 1956 and

I knew a lot about what you can and what you can't do with songs," said Howe in the Pollock book. "I said, look, the 5th Dimension would like to record 'Aquarius,' but I'd like to make it a medley and I'd like to use the last three bars of 'The Flesh Failures' and I don't want to do it without permission. So he said okay, you can go ahead and do it."

According to Howe, the song was plotted in the fall of 1968 and finished in January 1969. The Los Angeles session musicians known as The Wrecking Crew provided the instrumental backing for the song.

"I had to do a lot of work with my vocal arranger, Bob Alsivar. Because they couldn't sing both songs in the same key, we had to do a modulation; we figured out how I was going to do the instrumental arrangement so we could change keys," Howe told Pollack. "The record itself is the result of a conglomeration of things. I began as a jazz musician and I know the standard repertoire pretty well. I kept thinking about a song called 'Lost in the Stars' and trying to find something to give you that kind of impression. I described it to Bill Holman and he wrote that beautiful woodwinds and strings part that's in the intro. We did the track in L.A. and the vocals in Las Vegas where the 5th Dimension were opening for Frank Sinatra.

"We were working in that studio in Las Vegas where you used to have to stop when the train went by. Once when we were doing practice runs while the train passed, Billy started that riff at the end 'oh let the sunshine…' so I said, wait, let me put that on a separate track at the end. There were a lot of happy accidents making the record," said Howe in the book.

"When we went into the studio and recorded it, the group sang 'Let the sunshine in, let the sunshine in, the sun, shine in' over and over again. And then Bones told Billy, 'Now go in there and take it to church.' And Billy did. He went in there and went gospel on it," said McCoo.

Once the recording of the song was finished and members of the 5th Dimension heard the playback, they sensed that their initial impression was correct, that it would indeed become a hit for the group.

"We were right on that one," said Davis.

The single was a worldwide smash. It reached No. 1 on the U.S. Billboard Hot 100, the U.S. Billboard Pop Singles, the U.S. Billboard Adult Contemporary, and the Canada RPM Singles charts. It was No. 2 in Finland, No. 3 on both the German and Australian charts, No. 4 on the Swiss Singles chart and No. 11 in Austria and the United Kingdom.

"We knew it was special. But we had no idea it would end up doing what it did," said McCoo.

It was one of four singles released from the *Age of Aquarius* album that would make the Billboard charts. The other three were "Wedding Bell Blues," which was No. 1 on the adult contemporary and pop singles charts and No. 23 on the black singles chart; "Blowing Away," which made it to No. 7 on the adult contemporary chart and No. 21 on the pop singles chart; and "Workin' on a Groovy Thing," which went to No. 15 on the black singles chart and No. 20 on the pop singles chart.

"Wedding Bell Blues" provided some fun and memorable moments for Davis and McCoo.

The song was written and had been released by Laura Nyro. It had been a hit in California for her, but hadn't gotten much traction in the rest of the country.

"She wrote it for a guy named Bill in her life," said McCoo. "So when we started listening for material for the album, Bones suggested that I record it because Billy and I were going together at the time. Bones thought it would be a lark. So we said, 'Sure, why not?' We had no idea it would ever be a single."

A disc jockey in San Diego liked "Wedding Bell Blues" off the album and put it in his regular rotation of songs, and it got enough attention that Soul City recognized its potential and released it as the fourth single off the *Age of Aquarius* album and its second No. 1 hit.

"A lot of time the singles were picked off the album by DJs who were playing them and seeing what was getting the most reaction from listeners," said Davis.

Amidst the success of the album, McCoo and Davis would get married in July 1969. And soon thereafter the 5th Dimension would appear on *The Ed Sullivan Show* to sing "Wedding Bell Blues."

"That was a very special performance," said McCoo. "Every artist on *The Ed Sullivan Show* always did their performances live. But for that specific performance, they taped it because they had this concept in mind about Billy sneaking out of the room, trying to get away, and then they would have me show up outside the door. They had to tape it to get those special effects."

The 5th Dimension would continue releasing albums through 1975, but none as successful as *Age of Aquarius.* The group fared much better, however, with some of its singles during that period.

"One Less Bell to Answer" reached No. 2 on the Billboard Hot 100 Singles chart and No. 1 on the adult contemporary chart in 1970; a cover of The Association's "Never My Love" got to No. 12 on the Hot 100 chart and No. 1 on the adult contemporary chart in 1971; "(Last Night) I Didn't Get to Sleep at All" reached No. 8 on the Hot 100 and No. 2 on the Adult Contemporary chart in 1972; and "If I Could Reach You" got to No. 1 on the Hot 100 and No. 1 on the Adult Contemporary chart, also in 1972.

McCoo and Davis would leave the 5th Dimension in 1975, initially to pursue solo projects, but eventually deciding to become a duo. In 1976, they had a hit with "You Don't Have to be A Star (To Be In My Show)," which was a

No. 1 hit on both the U.S. Billboard Hot 100 Singles chart and the U.S. Billboard Hot Soul Singles chart.

The original quintet of McCoo — who also starred as host of the TV show *Solid Gold* in the 1980s — Davis, LaRue, Townson, and McLemore, reunited for the last time in 1990 and 1991 for a tour. After that, McCoo and Davis returned to be a duo and the others continued on their paths.

As of 2016, McCoo and Davis were still performing for adoring crowds and still having fun.

"The audiences have been just amazing. So supportive and excited. I don't want to say this because it sounds conceited, but they love everything that we're doing. And it's really special," said McCoo.

A few years ago, their former partner McLemore asked McCoo and Davis how long they were going to continue to perform.

"And we had told him, we love what we're doing. Why would we retire? You get onstage and the audiences are responding the way they're responding and they are so excited and loving everything we do," said McCoo. "We feel like, retire? Is he crazy?"

Billy Davis Jr. and his wife Marilyn McCoo were members of the 5th Dimension when Davis inadvertently left his wallet in a New York cab, which started a series of events that led to the 5th Dimension recording *Aquarius/Let the Sunshine* which became the group's most successful album. (Photo by Mike Morsch)

Discography

The 5th Dimension

"The Age of Aquarius"

Released May 1969

1. Medley: Aquarius/Let the Sunshine In (The Flesh Failures) (4:51) Galt MacDermot, James Rado, Gerome Ragni
2. Blowing Away (2:32) Laura Nyro
3. Skinny Man (2:51) Michael Kollander, Ginger Kollander
4. Wedding Bell Blues (2:44) Laura Nyro
5. Don't Cha Hear Me Callin' to Ya ( ) Rudy Stevenson
6. The Hideaway (2:45) Jimmy Webb
7. Workin' On a Groovy Thing (3:10) Roger Atkins, Neil Sedaka
8. Let It Be Me (3:54) Gilbert Bécaud, Mann Curtis, Pierre Delanoë
9. Sunshine of Your Love (3:18) Pete Brown, Jack Bruce, Eric Clapton
10. The Winds of Heaven (3:14) Bob Dorough, Fran Landesman
11. Those Were the Days (3:03) Gene Raskin
12. Let the Sunshine In (Reprise) (1:29) MacDermot, Rado, Ragni

Celebrating with Chicago Transit Authority

SUITABLE FOR FRAMING

Three Dog Night

(1969)

The members of Three Dog Night were in a real time crunch. They had about 35 days to find ten songs and record them for what would be their second album, *Suitable for Framing.*

The group, founded in 1967 by Danny Hutton, Cory Wells, Chuck Negron, Joe Schermie, Floyd Sneed, Jimmy Greenspoon, and Michael Allsup, had been a successful live act in Los Angeles and had signed with the Dunhill ABC label. The band's self-titled debut album, released in October 1968, had included the Top 5 hit single "One," written by Harry Nilsson.

The album itself had made it to No. 11 on the U.S. Billboard 200 Albums chart and was followed by a tour in support of the album. After that tour, record company officials were clamoring for the second album and wanted the band back in the studio. It was a frantic time.

In addition to those pressures, Hutton, Wells and Negron, the lead singers of the group, were considering adding yet another singer to the mix. And Hutton had his eye on a buddy of his, Danny Whitten, who was then with a band called the Rockets.

But Three Dog Night still needed songs to record for its next album and they needed them in a hurry.

Hutton recalled that Whitten had pitched him a song for the first album that Three Dog Night had initially passed on.

"Danny came up to my house and he had this demo tape with this song. Gary Bonner and Alan Gordon had written it and it was just gorgeous. But it was done with an orchestra with strings and horns," said Hutton. "Danny had brought it up for the first album and I just said there was no way we could do this live. This is a big, huge orchestrated thing.

"But we just didn't have that much time to work on the second album, so I said c'mon, let's do it and see if it works in the studio. And it worked," said Hutton.

The song was called "Celebrate" and it did indeed work in the studio. But it worked because Three Dog Night brought in the horn section of Chicago Transit Authority, who later shortened its name to Chicago, to make it work.

Jim Pankow, trombonist for Chicago Transit Authority, agreed to work with Three Dog Night on the recording of "Celebrate." (Photo by Mike Morsch)

Chicago Transit Authority was also a busy band. As Three Dog Night was looking for some studio help, CTA was recording what would be its self-titled debut album for Columbia Records.

Despite his full schedule, CTA trombonist Jim Pankow agreed to work with Three Dog Night on the recording of "Celebrate."

"Jim did those horn charts on that song. They came in, they heard the track and he just sat there and wrote the parts right there in the studio. He was very talented," said Hutton.

The CTA horn section would contribute to another song on the album, a cover of "Feelin' Alright," written by Dave Mason, from the band Traffic's eponymous 1968 album.

"Celebrate," with lead vocals by Hutton, would be one of three Top 20 hit singles for Three Dog Night off the *Suitable for Framing* album, which was released in June 1969. It would make it to No. 15 on the U.S. Billboard Hot 100 Singles chart and No. 8 on the Canadian Singles chart; "Eli's Coming," written by Laura Nyro with lead vocals by Wells, would get to No. 10 on the Billboard Singles chart and No. 4 on the Canadian Singles chart; and "Easy to Be Hard," written by Galt MacDermot, James Rado, and Gerome Ragni, with lead vocals by Negron, would go to No. 4 on the Billboard Singles chart and No. 2 on the Canadian Singles chart.

Chuck Negron was one of three lead singers that Three Dog Night used during the recording of the *Suitable for Framing* album. (Photo by Mike Morsch)

The song that Whitten had brought to Hutton did well for Three Dog Night, and Whitten himself was on a roll. In 1969, he and his band, the Rockets, began jamming with Neil Young, who had departed from his band, Buffalo Springfield, in 1968. For Young's second solo album, *Everybody Knows This Is Nowhere*, released in May 1969, Young had hired the Rockets as his band and changed the band's name to Crazy Horse. Whitten would be a guitarist and vocalist for Young on the album. Although Whitten was in a supporting role, he would sing co-lead with Young on the opening track of the album, "Cinnamon Girl."

But according to Hutton, Whitten was becoming a big-time heroin junkie. And his time with Crazy Horse was short. On Young's next solo effort, *After the Gold Rush,* Whitten and the rest of Crazy Horse were fired in the middle of the recording sessions, in part because of Whitten's heavy drug use.

Whitten died of a drug overdose on November 18, 1972, and his drug usage was part of what inspired Young to write the song "The Needle and the Damage Done," which appeared on Young's fourth studio album *Harvest,* released in February 1972.

There was one other song on *Suitable for Framing* that didn't garner much attention at the time, written by a couple of then-unknown songwriters.

When Three Dog Night had come off touring for its debut album and before the record company started pressuring the band to record its second album, Hutton had taken a few weeks off during the Christmas season of 1968 and traveled to London.

Knowing that the band was looking for songs, Hutton contacted DJM Records (Dick James Music), an independent British record label, once he got to London.

"I got ahold of the people at Dick James Music and said I was looking for songs for my group," said Hutton. "And they said, 'We'll send a writer over.' The guy they sent over, he was so sweet and such a nice guy."

The writer was Elton John.

Hutton and John decided to meet for the first time at a London club called Revolution. Elton planned to bring along his writing partner, Bernie Taupin.

"But Elton couldn't get into the club; the bouncer wouldn't let him in because his name wasn't on the guest list. I was really heartbroken," said Hutton. "There was a pub downstairs from the club, so Elton was there with Bernie. They were a little three sheets to the wind. We were just sitting there talking and Elton just started singing. And I said, 'My God, you've got a great voice.' And he said, 'Aw, I'm not really a singer. I just want to really write great songs.'"

Although Hutton didn't find any Elton John/Bernie Taupin songs he liked during that first meeting, John did send Hutton a demo tape that included two songs that Hutton received after he arrived back in Los Angeles. One of those songs, "Lady Samantha," did indeed end up on Three Dog Night's *Suitable for Framing* album, with lead vocals by Negron.

The other song on the demo was "Your Song." Three Dog Night liked that song as well, but didn't include it on the *Suitable for Framing* album, instead opting to use it on its fourth studio album, *It Ain't Easy*, released in March 1970.

"Your Song" didn't do anything for Three Dog Night, but around the same time, it was released as the B-side of Elton's single "Take Me to the Pilot." As was sometimes the case in those days, disc jockeys preferred the B-side song and flipped it over, giving "Your Song" extended airplay and making it a hit. It would become Elton's first pop hit, going to No. 8 on the Billboard Hot 100 Singles chart, and would appear on his self-titled second album, which was released the month after the Three Dog Night version of the song was released.

Elton John, along with songwriting partner Bernie Taupin, pitched some songs to Danny Hutton of Three Dog Night for the *Suitable for Framing* album, including one called "Your Song." Three Dog Night didn't choose any of those songs for the album, but would eventually record "Your Song" before John recorded it and made it a hit.
(Photo by Mike Morsch)

"The funny thing on 'Your Song' is that he sent it to me as a demo. But the little butthead didn't tell me that he was going to put it on his album. We did it first and then his album came out with it. So technically, he covered us," said Hutton.

The album cover for *Suitable for Framing* included a formal portrait of the three lead vocalists — Hutton, Wells, and Negron — looking straight-faced and wearing all black. But the photo on the inside of the album is a freak show.

All the band members are seen in the photo standing along a stream in a wooded area. And all are dressed in various over-the-top costumes, some with their faces painted. Also in the photo is a group of women, one of whom is pregnant and has the words "3 DOG NIGHT" painted on her stomach.

The photo was taken on Frank Zappa's property and the women were an a cappella group from the Los Angeles area called the GTOs (Girls Together Outrageously).

"I was friends with Frank Zappa. He lived down the street from me in a big old log cabin," said Hutton. "He had these crazy girls called the GTOs, who babysat for Frank and his wife. They were sweet girls, but all very wild and hippie and crazy. We met the girls and decided to do this crazy photo shoot. So everybody got dressed up and went out to Malibu for the shoot."

A couple of the girls, Pamela Miller and Christine Frka, were live-in nannies for Zappa's oldest child, Moon Unit.

Zappa encouraged their singing aspirations and had them open for his band, the Mothers of Invention, a few times. The GTOs recorded one album, *Permanent Damage* that was released in 1969 and produced by Zappa.

In the Three Dog Night photo, Pamela Miller is seen kneeling beside Cory Wells, her arm locked around his leg. Miller would go on to marry glam rocker Michael Des

Barres in 1977 and would eventually write two books about her experiences as a rock and roll groupie: *I'm With the Band* in 1987, in which she details affairs with Mick Jagger, Jimmy Page, Keith Moon, Waylon Jennings, Chris Hillman, and Jim Morrison; and *Take Another Little Piece of My Heart: A Groupie Grows Up* in 1993, which picks up where the first book ended, detailing Des Barres taking on motherhood and marriage, while making friends with stars like Don Johnson, Sylvester Stallone, Bob Dylan, and Dennis Hopper.

Suitable for Framing turned out to be a pretty strong second record for Three Dog Night. On the strength of the three hit singles, the album reached No. 16 on the U.S. Billboard 200 Albums chart and No. 15 on the Canadian Albums chart.

Hutton said he doesn't often revisit the albums he's done, but believes *Suitable for Framing* was a record that "sonically, it's well done."

Hutton believes the original group, together from 1968 to 1976, made some great music.

"I know I had a good time, but sometimes I don't remember why," he said.

Discography

Three Dog Night
"Suitable for Framing"

Released June 11, 1969

Side one

1. Feelin' Alright (3:39) Dave Mason
• Lead vocals shared by Hutton, Negron and Wells; includes the Chicago horn section.
2. Lady Samantha (2:53) Elton John, Bernie Taupin
• Lead vocal: Negron.
3. Dreaming Isn't Good for You (2:16) Danny Hutton
• Lead vocal: Hutton.
4. A Change Is Gonna Come (3:10) Sam Cooke
• Lead vocal: Wells.
5. Eli's Coming (2:41) Laura Nyro
• Lead vocal: Wells. Does not include the piano outro used in the 45 RPM mono mix of the song.

Side two

1. Easy to Be Hard (3:11) Galt MacDermot, James Rado, Gerome Ragni
• Lead vocal: Negron. Features an uncredited string section.
2. Ain't That a Lotta Love (2:16) Willie Dean "Deanie" Parker, Homer Banks
• Lead vocal: Wells.
3. King Solomon's Mines (2:29) Floyd Sneed
• Instrumental, dominated by percussion tracks performed by Sneed.
4. Circle for a Landing (2:20) Don Preston
• Lead vocal: Hutton.
5. Celebrate (3:13) Gary Bonner, Alan Gordon
• Lead vocals shared by Hutton, Negron and Wells; includes the Chicago horn section.

"We were going to be the next really big thing"

SELF-TITLED

Poco

(1970)

After the demise of Buffalo Springfield in the late 1960s, members Richie Furay and Jim Messina, along with the band's road manager, Rusty Young, decided to start a new group, a Southern California country rock band they called Poco.

But they needed a bass player.

Timothy B. Schmit was in the Sacramento-based band New Breed, which had changed its name to Glad and was recording the album *Feelin' Glad* in 1968.

"I had a friend, this girl, who knew some of the guys from Buffalo Springfield. She put it in their ear that I was around, and I auditioned for them," said Schmit. "They seemed to really like me and they asked me come back in two days. It turned out they had somebody else come in the following day."

That somebody else was Randy Meisner, and he had a similar story about how he found his way to an audition with Furay and Messina.

A friend, Buffalo Springfield's equipment manager Miles Thomas, had tipped Meisner that Furay and Messina were looking for a bass player. But Meisner remembers the audition a little differently.

Timothy B. Schmit wasn't chosen as the original bassist for Poco, but would eventually get the gig when Randy Meisner left the band. (Photo by Mike Morsch)

"After Miles told me that Jimmy Messina and Richie Furay were starting a group, they wanted me to do a tryout," said Meisner in a November 2016 interview with Ken Sharp for *Rockcellar* magazine. "I went out to Laurel Canyon and here's Timothy Schmit just walking out as I'm going in. I played for a while and they said, 'You're in.'"

Schmit believes he didn't get the job for a couple of reasons — primarily because Young, Poco drummer George Grantham, and Meisner were all from Denver, Colorado, and they already knew each other.

"The other thing was, there was a Selective Service issue on my part. So it was questionable as to whether I would be available," said Schmit.

Poco had risen out of the ashes of Buffalo Springfield, which had formed in 1966 with original members Furay, Stephen Stills, and Neil Young on guitar, Dewey Martin on drums, and Bruce Palmer on electric bass. Buffalo Springfield made its mark by helping pioneer the folk-rock genre.

The band experienced some lineup changes in its short history, with Messina first being a recording engineer and producer for the band, then eventually becoming the group's last bass player before it disbanded.

But Furay and Messina wanted to continue exploring new and different music genres after the Springfield implosion.

"We loved country music and we wanted to bridge the gap between rock and country," said Furay in an October 2015 online interview with Eddie Winters. "When the Springfield broke up, Jimmy was our last bass player and we became good friends. I really admired Jimmy and his talent and vision."

And that country rock genre was squarely in the crosshairs for Furay and Messina.

"There were other bands that were sort of doing it at the time," said Furay in the interview. "The Byrds were doing it, the Flying Burrito Brothers were doing it. We were doing it. We were pioneers; we were paving the way for a new sound and a new group. Jimmy's and my relationship at the time was absolutely focused and we knew what we wanted to do."

After the demise of Buffalo Springfield, Jim Messina would form Poco along with Richie Furay.
(Photo by Mike Morsch)

According to Messina, the first conversation that he recalls having with Furay about "what we wanted to do" was in a taxicab.

"He was bummed out that the band was busting up and we were on our last leg," said Messina in a May 2015 online interview with Eddie Winters. "My feeling was that having worked with all those great players, I already had a sense of what I was going to say: Instead of doing folk rock, we could do country rock. That kind of perked Richie's ear up. We just needed to get the right guys."

In Messina's mind, Poco was formed as an extension of what he and Furay were unable to finish with Buffalo Springfield.

"Unfortunately, we brought some of the same issues that stifled Buffalo Springfield. A lot of it was personality-inherent," Messina said in the interview with Winters.

The original members of Poco would include Furay, Messina, Young, Grantham, and Meisner.

The band's first album, *Pickin' Up the Pieces,* released in 1969, is considered a seminal album of the country rock genre. But it didn't perform that well on the charts, peaking at No. 63 on the U.S. Billboard 200 Albums chart.

And those internal personality problems that dogged Buffalo Springfield continued in Poco, and surfaced immediately after the recording sessions for *Pickin' Up the Pieces*.

During the mixing of the album, Meisner quit.

"Jimmy and Richie were in the studio. We'd finished the recording and had started the mix," said Meisner in the *Rockcellar* magazine interview. "I called down and said, 'I'd like to listen to it.'"

But according to Meisner, Furay said no, just he and Messina were going to mix the record.

"I said, 'Wait a minute, I made the music, too. I'd like to listen to the mixes.' But Richie said, 'No, just Jimmy and I are gonna do it.' So I said, 'If you're not gonna let me down there, I'm just gonna quit.' And it was simple as that," said Meisner in the magazine interview.

With Meisner's departure, Furay and Messina immediately turned to Schmit to be Poco's new bassist.

"Richie especially wanted me to be in the band, so I knew there must be something there," said Schmit. "It was exactly what I wanted to do at the time and it was doubly sweet because I had been originally turned down for the gig. I thought that it was my one and only chance to really do music at that level and that I blew it."

It would not be the last time that Schmit would replace Meisner in a band.

When Poco went into the studio to record its second album, the self-titled *Poco*, which would be released in 1970, Schmit said the band wanted someone who could not only play bass, but someone who was also a good singer and songwriter.

"I hadn't been much of a songwriter, but I always wanted to," said Schmit about that point in his career. "I told them I was good at all three — bass playing, singing and songwriting — so I started writing songs."

Of the seven songs on *Poco*, Schmit ended up co-writing "Keep on Believin'" with Furay.

"We just got together a few times and threw around some ideas for that song," said Schmit. "I learned a lot from Richie."

Once again, though, album sales were low. The record peaked at No. 58 on the U.S. Billboard 200 albums chart. However, the album did feature the Messina-penned song "You Better Think Twice," which did eventually become a signature song for the band.

Schmit sees Poco as part of the evolution of the country rock genre that already existed, citing the Everly Brothers, and Elvis Presley in his early days.

"We didn't have a super hit record, but this new thing was Poco, the Burrito Brothers, Pure Prairie League — that was kind of the evolution," said Schmit. "We knew a lot of people weren't doing it, but we also knew there was an audience for it. There was a lot of hype around Poco. We were going to be the next really big thing, but it didn't quite pan out that way. I was fortunate to sort of grab onto something that was already happening."

Messina would leave the band before the recording of Poco's fourth album, *From the Inside*. He would be replaced in October 1970 by Paul Cotton. Furay would leave the band in 1973.

Schmit would leave Poco in 1977 to join the Eagles, once again replacing Meisner as the band's bass player. Meisner, suffering from recurring stomach ulcers and struggling to hit the high notes on his signature song with the band, "Take It to the Limit," left the Eagles after the band's 11-month tour in support of its *Hotel California* album.

The Eagles went back into the studio to work on their next album, *The Long Run*, which would take two years to complete. But Schmit would make his mark immediately with the Eagles.

The Long Run, considered a disappointment by some critics at the time for failing to live up to *Hotel California*, was a commercial success.

When finally released in 1979, the album debuted at No. 2 on Billboard's Pop Albums chart, climbing to No. 1 just a week later, where it stayed for eight weeks.

The album, featured three Top 10 singles: "Heartache Tonight," written by Don Henley, Glenn Frey, Bob Seger, and J.D. Souther, reached No.1 on the U.S. Billboard Hot 100 singles chart and would win a Grammy for Best Rock Performance by a Duo or Group with Vocal; "The Long Run," written by Henley and Frey, which got to No. 8; and Schmit's first song for the group, "I Can't Tell You Why," on which he shared writing credit with Frey and Henley and which also got to No. 8 on the singles chart.

"Just being asked to be in the band was something special," said Schmit. "I continued to learn a whole lot, especially from Don and Glenn, about the craft of songwriting in general."

Schmit said he was happy that the band included "I Can't Tell You Why" rather than another country rock song on *The Long Run*.

"I'm a big fan of R&B and I was glad that for my debut as one of the Eagles, that song was more in that direction. I really liked that. I had no idea it would be on the charts."

But Henley did. Once *The Long Run* was completed, the band had a playback party for friends in Florida, where most of the album was recorded, at Bayshore Recording Studios in Coconut Grove.

"And when 'I Can't Tell You Why' came on, toward the end of the song, Don came over and whispered in my ear, 'There's your hit.' I kind of thought, well, I hope so," said Schmit.

The Long Run would be the last album the Eagles would make for Asylum Records. The band would break up for the first time in 1980.

After the breakup, Schmit embarked on a solo career and worked as a session bass player and backing vocalist. His voice can be heard on a number of hits, including Seger's "Fire Lake," "Look What You've Done to Me" by Boz Scaggs, and "Southern Cross" by Crosby, Stills, and Nash. He also toured with Toto and Jimmy Buffet in the 1980s, and was a member of Ringo Starr & His All-Starr Band in 1992.

Schmit has recorded six solo studio albums since 1984, the latest being *Leap of Faith,* which was released in 2016.

"I think all my solo albums are leaps of faith because you put out this stuff and you hope that people like it. I know I liked *Leap of Faith* and I suppose at this point in my career that's what matters more than anything. I want to keep going; I feel like I'm getting better and better at it and I'm enjoying touring as a solo artist. I didn't start that until late, within the last ten years," said Schmit.

"I don't have any illusions about making a hit record now. I write what I write and I record them and I enjoy it. It's my creative outlet these days."

Discography

Poco

Self-titled

Recorded October 1969 to February 1970
Released May 6, 1070

1. Hurry Up (4:06) Richie Furay
2. You Better Think Twice (3:21) Jim Messina
3. Honky Tonk Downstairs (2:43) Dallas Frazier
4. Keep on Believin' (2:51) Furay, Timothy B. Schmit
5 Anyway Bye Bye (7:01) Furay
6. Don't Let It Pass By (2:33) Furay
7. Nobody's Fool/El Tonto de Nadie, Regresa (18:25) Furay, Messina, George Grantham, Schmit, Young)

Brief interaction on the street launches Philly soul

SELF-TITLED
The Stylistics
(1971)

When Thom Bell and his songwriting partner, Linda Creed, couldn't come up with an idea for a song, they would leave their office and walk out into the streets of Center City Philadelphia.

There was always something in the streets to write about in the early 1970s.

On one of those times, Bell and Creed found themselves at Broad and Chestnut Streets, waiting to cross. When the light turned and the "walk" sign came on, the two songwriters and others started across the street.

When the group got into the intersection, Bell noticed that one guy had stopped and looked back. Then he went a few more steps, stopped, and looked back again. He was looking at a woman.

"And he called out this girl's name, hey so-and-so, but I couldn't hear the name," said Bell in a *Fresh Air* interview with Terry Gross on National Public Radio. "The girl looked at him like he was crazy. And he said, 'Oh, I'm sorry.' But he couldn't believe it wasn't who he thought it was.

"I was watching this and I said to Linda, 'I got an idea,'" said Bell.

When he got back to the office, he wrote the lyrics:

"Today I saw somebody,
who looked just like you.
She walked like you do,
I thought it was you.
As she turned the corner,
I called out your name.
I felt so ashamed,
when it wasn't you."

The interaction that Bell witnessed in the street and turned into a song would go on to be considered among the early soul landmark songs in the development of what would be called The Sound of Philadelphia (TSOP), also known as Philly soul. The song itself, "You Are Everything," would be one of the hits from the self-titled debut album, *The Stylistics,* released in 1971.

The Stylistics had been formed from two Philadelphia high school groups, the Percussions and the Monarchs. After high school, some members of each group continued on to higher education or went into military service.

Beverly Hamilton, an English teacher at Benjamin Franklin High School in Philadelphia, came up with the idea of taking the remaining members of both groups and forming a new one. Russell Thompkins, Jr., James Smith, and Airrion Love from the Monarchs, and James Dunn and Herbie Murrell from the Percussions, joined to become the Stylistics.

The new group worked locally for a few years and eventually recorded its first song, "You're a Big Girl Now," at Virtue Recording Studio in Philadelphia. The song became a No. 1 hit in Philadelphia, attracting the attention of Avco Records, which signed the group.

Record label officials at Avco wanted to follow up "You're a Big Girl Now" with an album by the Stylistics. And they wanted Bell — already a successful producer and songwriter

The group's self-titled debut album *The Stylistics* would be more of a solo effort that relied heavily on the high falsetto voice of Russell Thompkins Jr.
(Photo by Mike Morsch)

who had produced a catalogue of hits for the Delfonics, another Philadelphia group — who agreed, because he was impressed with the voice of Russell Thompkins, Jr., lead singer for the Stylistics.

A meeting between Bell and Thompkins was set.

"The record company sent me to a building in Philadelphia down on Broad Street to meet Tommy Bell. That morning I went down and met him and we sat around and we sang some. He started teaching me some songs, and that was the start of it," said Thompkins. "I thought he was a very talented man. When we sat down to sing, everything that I ended up doing on that album he could do. He played the music, he sang the songs."

Thompkins also recalls meeting Linda Creed that day. Creed and Thompkins weren't complete strangers, though.

"When she came into the room, I remembered that I had met Linda before. She was still a songwriter earlier in her career, but when I first met her, she was an artist. It must have been a good two years before that we had done a show together at a place in Philly called the Wynne Ballroom. So I was real fascinated seeing her working with Tommy at that time," said Thompkins.

What would become *The Stylistics* album, though, was more of a solo effort that relied heavily on the high falsetto voice of Thompkins, which is how Bell apparently wanted it, according to Thompkins.

"The one thing I can remember most of all was that it wasn't a Stylistics album, because the Stylistics didn't sing on that album," said Thompkins. "That album was done by Thom Bell, Linda Creed, myself, some background singers, along with some of the people [studio musicians] that were working at Philly International at that time. We did the work on that album. And the name Stylistics was put on it, I guess, mainly because I was there.

"It was a learning process for me at the time. When I went in there to do that album, I was only about nineteen or twenty years old," said Thompkins. "When you first start doing this stuff and you're recording music and learning, you have no idea what's going to be a hit. You have no idea that it's gonna be around for a long, long time. Things end up happening and there is a lot of luck involved."

In preparation for recording the album, Bell and Thompkins worked closely together, Bell as teacher and Thompkins as his willing and enthusiastic student.

"He had worked with a falsetto tenor before me, William Hart of the Delfonics. And Tommy also sang that way. He had a very high, natural voice, similar to Smokey Robinson. A lot of those songs he could have sung and recorded himself. He had the same type of voice," said Thompkins. "When I sat down at the piano with him, he could show me everything. He would sing the songs to me and just from listening to him, I knew whether I could do them or not."

At the time, Thompkins was using what he called "a different voice" than what Bell would end up wanting on the album.

"One of the first things he told me when we started working was, 'I'm gonna bring that voice down.' I used to sing much higher than that. And he brought me down to a different key to sing in," said Thompkins. "At the time, I was happy about it and not happy about it. But it fit. I became very happy about when I got older because my voice changed. Now, I'm still able to sing in that key. I don't know if he knew that was gonna happen then, but it was a gift that he gave me."

The album would be recorded from late 1970 and through 1971 at Sigma Sound Studios in Philadelphia and released on November 6, 1971. It would include the group's first hit, "You're a Big Girl Now," which would be re-

released as the album's first single. But Bell and Creed had written some other very good songs to fill out the record.

The first one recorded, and the second single released from the album, was "Stop, Look, Listen," on which Bell implemented some techniques that he had perfected with the Delfonics. And he added those to an arrangement that complemented the falsetto voice of Thompkins. That song would reach No. 6 on the U.S. Billboard Hot R&B chart and No. 39 on the U.S. Billboard Hot 100 Singles chart.

The third single from the album was "You Are Everything," and although that was a special song for Bell, Thompkins was less enthusiastic about it.

"I didn't like that one," said Thompkins. "It was years later that Tommy told me that was a very special song for him. It was something that he saw walking down the street that made him think of those lyrics. Another songwriter friend of mine, Charlie Simmons, used to tell me that he'd get on the C bus in Philly and ride from one end to the other and just look out the window to see what people were doing. And he would get inspired to write something. That's how songwriters are. And 'You Are Everything' was special for Tommy."

The fourth single from the album was "Betcha By Golly, Wow," which had been recorded in 1970 by Connie Stevens under a different title, "Keep Going Strong." Bell believed that with Thompkins on the lead vocal, the song could become a hit.

"In the history of songwriters, there have been many songs written with the words 'I love you' and there are a lot of different versions of those same words or a reasonable facsimile of those words," said Bell in the NPR interview. "But there's only one 'Betcha By Golly, Wow' in history, because I was the only one crazy enough to write something like that. All of those words are an expression of surprise. 'Golly,' 'gee,' 'wow' and similar words. They were elements of expressions. So I wondered, hmmm, can I put those together and come up with a concept? So that's where that came from."

Thompkins loved "Betcha By Golly, Wow" the first time he heard it.

"That's my favorite Stylistics song. I never get tired of singing it," he said. "I knew from the beginning that I wanted to sing everything Tommy and Linda gave me. It was like it was made for me. I loved to sing those songs. They were easy to sing."

"Betcha By Golly, Wow" would get to No. 2 on the R&B chart and No. 3 on the Hot 100 Singles chart.

The album itself would reach No. 23 on the U.S. Billboard Top LPs chart and No. 3 on the U.S. Billboard Top Soul LPs chart. It is considered a "sweet soul landmark" that was instrumental in establishing The Sound of Philadelphia (TSOP).

Being in on the ground floor of the Philly soul sound also created some challenges for groups like the Stylistics. There was a lot of competition in Philadelphia at the time, and it was being driven in large part by Kenny Gamble and Leon Huff, producers and songwriters who established Philadelphia International Records (PIR).

Though not a business partner in Philadelphia International with Gamble and Huff, out of necessity, Bell was a partner with them in the Mighty Three Music publishing company, according to a *Billboard* magazine story from 2006.

"I was producing for one side of Philadelphia, and Gamble was producing for another side of Philadelphia. And we found that we had a better chance, did much better if we joined forces. He had his sound, I had my sound, but put it together and the sound worked perfectly," said Bell in the magazine interview.

"In those days, you didn't have your own publishing company. You had to go with the big white companies and they owned all the stuff. If you wrote something, they would take the publishing and we didn't like that. So they'd say, 'If you don't do it our way, we won't record your stuff.' So we said, 'We'll try our way,'" said Bell.

Bell also liked the independence of working with different artists, which enabled him to make records with the Delfonics at Philly Groove Records and the Stylistics on Avco Records.

"I was not involved [as a business partner] in Philadelphia International, and since that was the case, I was an independent producer," he said in the magazine interview. "I didn't even produce most of the PIR artists. I did the outside stuff. Gamble & Huff were building PIR; I was building Bell Boy Productions. It all funneled into Mighty Three Music, the songwriter mechanicals and royalties."

But the artists themselves working in the Philly soul scene in the 1970s could feel the pressure to make their mark.

"I felt competition from Day One when the group became professional. There were so many singing groups in Philadelphia then," said Thompkins. "I remember getting my butt whipped by a couple of the groups the first time I ever worked with them. And if I was going to work with them again, I was coming back with new ammunition. You got me once, you're not going to get me again."

One of the things that Thompkins did to set himself and the Stylistics apart from other groups was something that a lot of the other male singers wouldn't do, and that was sing songs normally performed by female artists. He believed his voice was suited for those songs.

"I would sing Aretha Franklin, I would sing Dionne Warwick, things that other singers didn't do," said Thompkins. "A lot of people were really fascinated by that and I used that as a weapon to set myself apart. I learned a lot from listening to those artists and I would put those songs in the show."

Bell would end up working with the Stylistics for three albums, and he and Creed would write additional hits for the group, including "I'm Stone in Love With You," "Break Up to Make Up," "Rockin' Roll Baby," and "You Make Me Feel Brand New," which would get to No. 2 on the U.S. Billboard Hot 100 Singles chart.

Bell had started producing and writing for the Spinners in 1973 and had a run of hit singles and albums with that group through 1976. He ended his collaboration with the Stylistics in 1974.

The Stylistics began to struggle after Bell's departure in 1974. They had trouble finding the right material and by 1976 had switched labels to H&L Records. By 1978, the chart successes for the Stylistics were gone.

Thompkins remained a part of the Stylistics through 2000, but finally left the group that year.

"There was a period between 1973 up until about 2000 where there were problems with us not being on the same page and not making the music together and the way we got along," said Thompkins. "That became very hurtful. And it grew because I chose to stay with the group instead of leaving when I thought I should have. Around 2000, I couldn't stand it anymore and I had to leave."

He now performs as Russell Thompkins, Jr. and the New Stylistics. But he's happy with the legacy of the Stylistics and the music that the group made that helped them establish themselves as the early pioneers of The Sound of Philadelphia.

"I'm proud that I did go into the studio and work with people like Tommy Bell and a lot of gifted musicians and artists in Philadelphia to create things. And I'm very proud about the fact that I came from the ghettos of Philadelphia and had a chance to travel all over the world and work with some great people. I've been very fortunate in my life," he said.

Discography

The Stylistics
Self-titled
Released Nov. 6, 1971

All tracks written by Thom Bell and Linda Creed, except where noted.
Side one
1. Stop, Look, Listen To Your Heart (2:54)
2. Point of No Return (2:45)
3. Betcha by Golly, Wow (3:47)
4. Country Living (2:57)
5. You're a Big Girl Now (3:14) Marty Bryant, Robert Douglas

Side two
6. You Are Everything (2:55)
7. People Make the World Go Round (6:26)
8. Ebony Eyes (2:21)
9. If I Love You (2:05)

Some big names help make a big album

NO SECRETS

Carly Simon

(1972)

They just couldn't get it. Carly Simon, Bonnie Bramlett, Doris Troy, and Jimmy Ryan were doing backup vocals for "Night Owl," a James Taylor song that Simon planned to use on her third studio album, *No Secrets*.

"But it wasn't going anywhere. We just weren't coming up with anything great," said Ryan, who was Simon's guitarist on the album.

Jimmy Ryan was the lead guitarist and backing vocalist on Carly Simon's *No Secrets* album. (Photo by Mike Morsch)

The recording sessions were done in September and October 1972 at Trident Studios in London, England. Many Apple Records artists used Trident Studios, including Taylor, Badfinger, and Billy Preston. Ringo Starr had recorded "It Don't Come Easy" there, and part of

George Harrison's 1970 album *All Things Must Pass* was recorded at Trident.

Simon was working for the first time with producer Richard Perry on the *No Secrets* album, and Perry was a pretty well-established producer by 1972. He was connected to a lot of big-name recording artists.

So to have Bonnie Bramlett, of Delaney and Bonnie, and Doris Troy, who co-wrote and recorded "Just One Look" — which reached No. 10 on the U.S. Billboard Hot 100 Singles chart in 1963 — singing backup on the *No Secrets* album, wasn't unusual.

"At Trident Studios it was just pick your all-star band for any one of those cuts. It was ridiculous who Carly and Richard pulled in. Based on her credibility at that point, everyone wanted to play with her. There were no problems getting together an all-star team," said Ryan.

But Simon, Bramlett, Troy, and Ryan just weren't clicking on "Night Owl." Something was missing. And everybody knew it.

In the control booth, Perry wasn't hearing it, either. He'd lean on the talk-back button and say, "Not quite, guys. Give it another try. Try something else; it's not quite working."

The four singers did several takes, and finally did get one that they thought was OK. But after that take, they didn't hear anything from Perry.

"We were waiting to hear what he said, and I looked into the control room and I noticed he was talking to somebody, being distracted," said Ryan. "I look and, oh my God, it's Paul McCartney. Paul McCartney is in the studio. And Carly goes, '*What?*' We both looked at each other and said, 'Whoa.'"

McCartney looked through the glass, waved to the singers, and hit the talk-back button. "I hear you're having a little trouble with your backup vocals. Would you like a little help?"

From Paul McCartney? Well, yes.

"Paul came out and started singing with us. In seconds he came up with the part that we needed, as I'm sure he did with the Beatles," said Ryan. "The guy is just a monster talent."

Perry got the take he was looking for and "Night Owl" was finished for that session.

But that wasn't the end of the evening for some of those in the studio. After the session, the group was standing around chatting. At some point, Bramlett and Troy went home, leaving Simon, Ryan, Perry, and McCartney in the studio.

"I don't recall if Linda [McCartney] was there; she might have been. So Paul just kind of drops it that he got called to write the theme song for a movie and he wasn't sure whether it was any good," said Ryan. "So he said, 'Do you want to hear it? Can I play it for you?' And he sits down at the piano and he plays, 'Live and Let Die.'

"Other than George Martin and I guess the members of Wings, we were the first people in the world to hear this song," said Ryan. "I was standing there quietly with my hand at my side pinching myself. Am I really hearing Paul McCartney playing a song that no one else has heard, that's about to be recorded?"

"Live and Let Die," the theme for the 1973 James Bond movie of the same name, and written by Paul and Linda McCartney, made it to No. 2 on the U.S. Billboard Hot 100 Singles chart for McCartney and his band, Wings. It was the first James Bond theme song to be nominated for an Academy Award for Best Original Song, but lost that year to the theme song from *The Way We Were*, sung by Barbra Streisand.

It was like that for the *No Secrets* album. Carly Simon was smoking hot by 1972. The title track on her second album, *Anticipation*, released in 1971, had reached No. 3 on the U.S. Billboard Adult Contemporary chart and No. 13 on the U.S. Billboard Hot 100 Singles chart.

Not only that, but her personal life had heated up as well. She had supplanted Joni Mitchell as the primary love interest in James Taylor's life, and although the two had not yet married, they were heavily involved by the time Simon started recording the *No Secrets* album.

Ryan had watched much of Simon's personal and professional life unfold. The two had met a few years earlier when Ryan, fresh off the breakup of his band the Critters, which had a Top 25 hit in 1966 called "Mr. Dieingly Sad," needed work and took a job at a guitar store in Greenwich Village owned by a guy named Dan Armstrong, who had also produced the Critters.

Simon was Armstrong's girlfriend at the time, and she'd regularly hang out at the store.

A few years later, when Simon got her first record deal, she asked Ryan to play on her first album, the self-titled *Carly Simon,* released in February 1971. Ryan also played on the *Anticipation* album and was heavily involved with the *No Secrets* album.

And *No Secrets* would end up featuring what would eventually become Simon's signature song and one that's considered by Billboard as one of the Greatest Songs of All-Time: "You're So Vain."

According to Simon's 2015 memoir *Boys in the Trees*, the song was originally called "Bless You, Ben" and then "Ballad of a Vain Man" and was about "a man who owned a yacht, a private jet, a hat that comes over one eye, and an expensive horse that ran at Saratoga, who had the ability to do French parlor dances, had some friends in the underworld and who'd obviously had some extramarital dalliances."

Simon wrote that during the recording sessions, which eventually moved to AIR Studios, she and Perry had done "a hundred takes of the basic track and at least thirty lead vocals for what we called 'Ballad of a Vain Man.'"

But another big-name guest artist was about to make an appearance on backing vocals.

"Richard had asked me to do the harmony parts while a 'circle of friends,' as he called them (I called them highly intimidating musicians), listened," wrote Simon. "I begged Harry Nilsson to sing with me, and he didn't hesitate to accept. Harry was a close friend of John Lennon's and was one of the terrific artists who didn't promote his work by stage performance. He was handsome and tall, wearing sunglasses, and had tawny hair curling around his unmistakable face. We were comfortable enough with each other, and got in a few takes (which means fewer than 25 with Richard at the helm) before I got a call on the studio phone and stepped out to take it in the lounge.

"'Hallow, is this Caughly?' I didn't have to ask who it was."

It was Mick Jagger.

"'How did you know I was here? Had Mick ever not been able to find anybody?" wrote Simon. "I told him I was putting some vocals on a track with Harry and invited him to come."

According to Simon, Jagger was at the studio almost immediately.

"It's pretty easy, Mick," wrote Simon. "Just sing the melody if you feel like it, or improvise and do any harmony you think of.

"I remember that after four or five perfect go-rounds, Harry said, 'You two do not need me, you sound as though you're joined at the hip.' He left for the control booth to find his future in a drink.

"As we sang together — Mick was a natural at singing backup — the energy was choreographed by the heavens, an unexpected fever that was certainly heightened by the music. The song that had been waiting to come to life for so long finally exploded," wrote Simon.

"It was shortly after midnight. Mick and I, we were close together — the same height, same coloring, same lips. I could feel him, eyes wide on me. I felt as if I were trying to stay within a pink gravity that was starting to loosen its silky grip on me. I was thrilled by the proximity, remembering all the times I had spent imitating him in front of my closet mirror. Only now we were both Narcissus, each desiring our reflection in the other; I was moving in step with him. Not trying to, but Richard gave us directions that seemed more football coach than record producer: 'Mick, step back just a bit, your voice cuts more than Carly's. Try doubling your parts and stand a little further away, both of you.'

"The farther away we stood, the closer we got. Electricity. That's what it was. I wanted to touch his neck and he was looking at my lips. The electricity was raw and hardly disguising its power. Having sex would have actually cooled things off," wrote Simon.

Ryan wasn't in the studio that evening to witness that electricity between Simon and Jagger.

"Carly never let anybody in when she was doing lead vocals," said Ryan. "I wouldn't say she was nervous, but she felt she did better in an intimate situation when it was just her, the producer and the engineer. If people were sitting there watching, she got self-conscious and all that."

With the exception of Jagger, apparently.

According to Ryan, Jagger had visited the studio many times during the making of *No Secrets*.

"He was working on something with the Stones in another studio nearby. Mick is a big social kind of guy, so he bounces around looking for whatever," said Ryan.

But after the vocal recording sessions on "You're So Vain" were done, Simon called Ryan and asked him if he wanted to hear the playback.

"So she played it for me and I go, 'Whoa, Carly, why are you trying to sound like Mick Jagger?' She's got this shit-eating grin on her face and said, 'Listen to it again.' "And again, I said, 'Oh man, you really sound like Mick Jagger. How did you do that?' And she said, 'It's him. He wandered into the studio,'" said Ryan, who plays the lead guitar on "You're So Vain."

The song also has a unique intro, courtesy of bassist Klaus Voormann, who had brought a huge bass guitar called a guitarron to the recording sessions.

Voormann, an accomplished flamenco guitarist, was fooling around with the guitarron during a break in one session, showing Ryan some things on the instrument.

Perry overheard what Voormann was playing and liked it.

"Let's make that the beginning of the song," Ryan recalls Perry saying to Voormann. And that's the bass lead-in one hears on the record, with Simon whispering "son of a gun."

After keeping it a secret for more than 40 years, Simon does admit in her book that "You're So Vain" is indeed about actor Warren Beatty. But only the second verse.

"And no, the song is not just about one person," wrote Simon in *Boys in the Trees*. "Let's just say that Warren Beatty played second base in this particular infield, which he knows so well, but as for who manned first and third — ask the shortstop. In all seriousness, the subjects of the first and third verses don't know that this song is also about them, so it would be inappropriate and a rude awakening to disclose their identities until they, them (vain) selves, were notified."

Ryan, though, believes he may have sensed long before anyone else that part of the song was about Beatty. That's because he once unknowingly threw Beatty out of Simon's dressing room in the early 1970s.

Carly and the band were playing at the Troubadour in West Hollywood, California, and prior to the performance, were hanging out in the dressing room when there came a knock at the door.

"There's this guy wearing one of those flammable rayon goofy shirts and he had on huge glasses," said Ryan. "He said, 'Hi, I'd like to see Carly.' I didn't recognize him, he was just this goofy guy who wanted to barge into the dressing room. I said, 'Dude, we're about to go on. Maybe come to the stage door afterwards. And he said, 'No, I'd like to see her now.' I said, 'Forget it' and slammed the door in his face.

"I turned around and Carly had her hands over her mouth. She said, 'Oh my God, do you know who that was that you just slammed the door on?' I said, 'It was just some dweeby guy. Who? What?' And she said, 'It was Warren Beatty.' I said, 'Oh no, let me go get him' and she said, 'No, no, no. Leave it. That's so perfect. That's exactly what he needed,'" recalled Ryan.

"That always gave me the impression that's where the birth of 'You're So Vain' was. Whether or not it was, she wouldn't tell me because it was her closely guarded secret. But that was my impression," said Ryan.

No Secrets became Simon's commercial breakthrough album. Released on November 28, 1972 by Elektra Records, it spent five weeks at No. 1 on the U.S. Billboard 200 Albums chart. "You're So Vain" was a monster smash, spending three weeks at No. 1 on the U.S. Billboard Hot 100 Singles chart and two weeks at No. 1 on the Billboard Adult Contemporary chart.

The album was nominated for four Grammys in 1974: Record of the Year, Song of the Year, Best Pop Vocal Performance, Female, and Best Engineered Recording but didn't win in any of those categories. The song itself is ranked No. 72 on Billboard's Greatest Songs of All-Time list.

Ryan calls Simon's *No Secrets* his "favorite album of all time that she did."

"I loved every song on it. And the experience of playing with guys like Klaus Voormann and Jim Gordon and Nicky Hopkins from the Rolling Stones and Bobby Keys from the Rolling Stones, and Lowell George from Little Feat and [session drummer] Jim Keltner. It seems the better the musicians are, the more human they are. They're the nicest people and just so professional," said Ryan. "When you do sessions with guys who are that good, there is no such thing as a bad take. There's only a take that isn't quite what the artist or producer is looking for."

After the *No Secrets* album, Ryan moved to England for a time, which limited his relationship with Simon. He played some random dates with her over the years, but mostly she would call him only for recording sessions. In recent years, Ryan has been part of The Hit Men, a group of professionals who have played and recorded with some of the biggest names in the industry over the years, including Simon, McCartney, Frankie Valli, and Elton John.

As for *No Secrets*, Ryan wasn't surprised at all that the album propelled Simon to the next level of music stardom.

"There was always something very unique about Carly," he said. "She was a sensational songwriter and she was writing really good songs then. So the combination of looking that good, writing great songs and having a very unusual voice — like it or hate it, it didn't sound like anybody else at the time — Carly truly stood out. She didn't sound like anybody else. Those things gave her a leg up."

Discography

Carly Simon

"No Secrets"

Released Nov. 28, 1972

All songs written by Carly Simon, unless otherwise noted.

Side one

1. The Right Thing to Do (2:57)

2. The Carter Family (3:29) Simon, Jacob Brackman

3. You're So Vain (4:17)

4. His Friends Are More Than Fond of Robin (3:00)

5. We Have No Secrets (3:57)

Side two

1. Embrace Me, You Child (4:06)

2. Waited So Long (4:14)

3. It Was So Easy (3:06) Simon, Brackman

4. Night Owl (3:47) James Taylor

5. When You Close Your Eyes (3:05) Simon, Bill Mernit

The surfer who bailed on the sailor

CARL AND THE PASSIONS "SO TOUGH" AND HOLLAND

The Beach Boys

(1972 and 1973)

By 1971, Brian Wilson was suffering from mental illness and drug abuse and his contributions to the Beach Boys were limited. (Photo by Mike Morsch)

After spending about three months recording in Holland over the summer of 1972, the Beach Boys had returned to the United States thinking they had finished their 19th studio album.

But when they presented the album, called *Holland*, to Warner Brothers, record company officials rejected it because it didn't appear to the suits that it had a song that could be marketed as a potential hit single.

Beach Boys co-founder Brian Wilson had co-written another song — along with Van Dyke Parks, Ray Kennedy, Tandyn Almer, and Jack Rieley — that Parks, then the director of audio-visual services at Warner Brothers and a longtime collaborator of Brian Wilson, thought might allay the concerns of record company officials.

The thinking was that the song "We Got Love," which record company officials considered the weakest of the tracks on the *Holland* album, could be replaced with the new song, which could then be released as a single.

Blondie Chaplin would contribute a song and vocals for the Beach Boys' *Carl and the Passions – So Tough* album and would sing lead on "Sail On, Sailor" for the group's *Holland* album. (Photo by Mike Morsch)

So Brian Wilson's brothers, Carl and Dennis, along with guitarist Blondie Chaplin and drummer Ricky Fataar, went back into the studio in Los Angeles and recorded the song.

Chaplin and Fataar, both South African natives who were with a band called the Flames, had joined the Beach Boys in 1971 at Carl Wilson's invitation. He had hoped to infuse some new blood into the band that in the early 1970s was trying to remake its image and struggling to maintain its relevance.

"On the original track I played bass, Ricky played drums, and Carl was on the electric piano. It was just the three of us," said Chaplin. "Then Carl asked Dennis to sing the lead. Dennis took one pass — not even a pass really — and said 'Carl, this is not for me. It doesn't sound good for me. And by the way, the surf is up and I'm going surfing.' That was it. It wasn't weird or anything, it was just Dennis. He just said, 'Hey, I'm going to surf now.'

"Then Carl sang it, and it sounded good to me. But he didn't like the timbre of his voice on it. So he asked me to give it a shot.

"I sang it twice and that's what you hear on the album. That's how I got a chance to sing it," said Chaplin.

The song was "Sail On, Sailor," and it was released as a single off the *Holland* album in 1973. The album itself was critically well received, peaking at No. 36 in the U.S. on the Billboard 200 Albums chart and No. 20 on the United Kingdom Top 40 Albums chart.

"Sail On, Sailor" only made it to No. 79 on the U.S. Billboard Hot 100 Singles chart when it was first released. But it was re-released two years later, in 1975, and reached No. 49 on the Billboard Hot 100 Singles chart.

Chaplin's contributions to the Beach Boys had actually started with the band's 18th studio album, *Carl and the Passions — "So Tough,"* which was released on May 15, 1972, right before the Beach Boys departed for Holland to record the 19th album.

Carl and the Passions is a reference to a pre-Beach Boys group that Brian Wilson had put together with his cousin Mike Love. To entice his younger brother Carl to join the group, Brian named it Carl and the Passions for a performance at Hawthorne High School in southern California, where the Wilson brothers went to high school.

Another Hawthorne High student, Al Jardine, was in the audience for that show and was impressed by what he heard from Carl and the Passions.

By 1971, Brian Wilson was suffering from mental illness and drug abuse and his contributions to the Beach Boys were limited.

Carl Wilson had stepped in as the group's de facto leader and wanted to shake up the structure of the band by bringing in Chaplin and Fataar.

"I think how it really went, Al [Jardine] came to see us first and then he called Carl to come see this great band. Then Carl came to see us and loved the band," said Chaplin.

The Flames eventually flamed out and had disbanded by the end of 1970, which left the door open for Chaplin and Fataar to join the Beach Boys when offered the chance by Carl Wilson.

In his 2016 autobiography *Good Vibrations: My Life as a Beach Boy,* Mike Love wrote that Chaplin and Fataar were welcome additions to the Beach Boys.

"Not only were they good musicians, but their presence itself was a statement. Formerly living under apartheid, they integrated the Beach Boys, bringing us greater diversity in race and sound," wrote Love.

Chaplin and Fataar would end up contributing two songs on the "*So Tough*" album: "Here She Comes" and "Hold On Dear Brother."

"'Hold On Dear Brother,' that's a real good song; the other one is 'Here She Comes.' Those were good songs," said Chaplin. "Ricky and I wrote those awhile prior to that. Carl wanted to open the club up a bit, so to speak, and asked us if we wanted to contribute a couple of songs [to the album]. He was very open as far as trying to get some new blood. That's what we were."

Working with the Beach Boys also afforded Chaplin the opportunity to observe the Wilson brothers up close, despite the minimal participation of Brian Wilson.

Brian had three writing credits on the "*So Tough*" album: "You Need a Mess of Help to Stand Alone," the first song on Side One that he co-wrote with Jack Rieley, who was also managing the Beach Boys; "He Come Down," on which he shared writing credit with Love and Jardine; and "Marcella," on which he shared writing credit with Rieley and Tandyn Almer.

"The drugs had different effects. Acid was something else because it put voices in my head. That was a bad drug. I'm sorry I did it," Brian wrote in his 2016 autobiography, *I Am Brian Wilson.* "I liked Seconals, downers — they were a relax pill. Cocaine came along in the late '60s, maybe 1969. When I wrote 'Sail On, Sailor,' there was coke around. I also co-wrote, with Al and Mike, 'He Come Down,' which sounded like it was about the end of a drug trip but was really more of a gospel thing. I love that tune. Mike's lead is so soulful."

"Brian usually was the main thrust of stuff. Just like any brothers, they were very close, but also, as you can tell, completely and radically different," said Chaplin. "Whatever Brian's radically different things were at the time, people have documented that, they combined with the candor of Dennis and with Carl being the peacemaker. Three different personalities, and that's how it was.

"Bands are always like that; there are always different personalities. One guy is a little weird, one guy is a little bit nice or whatever. But blended together, they make a good sound.

"Now if you pull them all apart, you go holy shit. But put them together, it's just like magic. That's what usually happens in the good bands and the world gets to see that creative spark," said Chaplin.

Apparently, though, *Rolling Stone* magazine wasn't impressed with the creative spark — or lack thereof — on *Carl and the Passions — "So Tough."* Nor was it impressed with the contributions on the album from Chaplin and Fataar.

In a review published on June 22, 1972, writer Stephen Davis recognized the limited role of Brian Wilson on the album and the fact that he had "abdicated the leadership of the organization into the capable hands of brother Carl."

Davis was unkind to Chaplin and Fataar. He wrote: "The two Chaplin/Fataar tunes are derivative and boring. 'Here She Comes' sounds like Traffic. 'Hold on Brother' sounds like The Band with pedal-steel guitar thrown in. Execrable."

Davis was more kind about at least one of Brian Wilson's contributions. "'Marcella' is in the classic mold of the best of Brian's parking lot rockers, capturing the synthesis of the 'So Tough' ambience of the pom-pom playgirl, the new girl in school, the 1972 Rhonda. This babe is set off by glistening synthesized effects, rhythmic chimes, and Mike Love's familiar, tough vocal poses and struts; 'You Need a Mess of Help to Stand Alone' is the only other Brian Wilson/Jack Rieley effort, and why it was released as the single instead of the bejeweled 'Marcella,' to which it can't hold the proverbial candle, is known only to some incompetent loon in Burbank."

Overall, though, Davis was disappointed with the album. "'*So Tough's'* insurmountable problem is that only four of the eight cuts fall into the subtly specialized class of 'acceptable' Beach Boy material. It was, at least, honest to call the band Carl and the Passions. Because the difference is Brian, and the difference hurts."

Mike Love agreed.

"The album was a disjointed rush job, hastily assembled between live gigs, that even Carl admitted was weak overall," wrote Love in his book. "More than anything, the record emphasized how confused we were about our brand. Warner/Reprise released it as half of a double LP set, coupled with *Pet Sounds*. The Beach Boys, as part of a settlement with Capitol Records, had the rights to our LPs from after 1965 to 10 years, so someone at Warner/Reprise had the bright idea of coupling *Carl and the Passions – 'So Tough'* with *Pet Sounds*, undermining the whole makeover strategy."

Despite the critical reviews, the Beach Boys left for Holland and went right back to work on the next album. Chaplin and Fataar remained with the band and contributed on that album as well, co-writing the song "Leaving This Town" with Carl Wilson.

"It was great to be in Holland for three months just trying to make some music. It was a good album," said Chaplin. "I just know one thing: I've always felt that Carl got us in there for new blood and was willing to go and give it a shot to make something new go down, develop a new kind of personality for the band. The album had some problems when it first came out because record company officials couldn't find a hit song.

"But 'Sail On, Sailor' was it. We cut 'Sail On, Sailor' and put it on the album so we could have a little bit of wings on the radio. That's how that came about. But now when you listen to it as a whole album, it plays pretty good," said Chaplin.

This time, a different reviewer for *Rolling Stone* agreed.

"In acknowledgment of Brian Wilson's still honored, if slightly mythological, status, even within the group, the album both opens and closes with a new Brian opus. As usual, each is informed by a singular sensibility that, currently, seems inclined toward a kind of chamber rock," wrote Jim Miller in the *Rolling Stone* review first published on March 1, 1973. "Blondie Chaplin's superb vocal on 'Sail On, Sailor' situates that song between recent Stevie Wonder and vintage Beach Boys, although the expansive harmonies and insistent triplets ultimately assert the group's own rights."

Miller continued: "Like the finest Beach Boys' work, *Holland* makes me consistently smile, as much at its occasionally unnerving simplicity of viewpoint as at its frequently ornate perfection. Although the Beach Boys may be an acquired taste, once the listener has granted them their stylistic predilections, their best records become irresistible. Their music long ago transcended facile categorization, and they now play what might as well be described simply as Beach Boys music. Unlike last year's disappointing '*So Tough,' Holland* offers that music at its most satisfying. It is a special album."

There was one other dynamic going on with the Beach Boys during the recording of these two albums after Bruce Johnston, who had become Brian's permanent replacement in the touring band in the mid-1960s, left the band in 1972.

"Tension within the band continued to simmer. No one admired Brian's music talents more than Bruce Johnston, but Bruce stayed clear of drugs and was increasingly frustrated by their effects on all of my cousins," wrote Love in his autobiography. "One day, when he was recording at Brian's home studio, Bruce posted a sign on the door: 'No Wilsons allowed.' And soon there would be no Johnston either. With the support of Jack Rieley, the Wilsons voted Bruce out of the band in 1972."

Johnston's only contribution on *Carl and the Passions – "So Tough"* is as a background vocalist on the song "Marcella." He did not make the trip to Holland and wouldn't rejoin the Beach Boys until 1978.

Chaplin would leave the Beach Boys in 1976. He recorded a self-titled solo album for Asylum Records in 1977 and, in the 1980s, toured with The Band. In the 1990s,

Chaplin was a guitarist, backing vocalist, and percussionist for the Rolling Stones, both on tour and in the studio.

More than 40 years after recording the "*So Tough*" and *Holland* albums, Chaplin rejoined Brian Wilson and Al Jardine on an extended tour that celebrated the 50th anniversary of Brian's masterpiece *Pet Sounds* album. During that tour, Chaplin had the opportunity to once again sing "Sail On, Sailor" live, even though the song appeared on the *Holland* album and not the *Pet Sounds* album. Brian Wilson used the song as an opportunity to salute Chaplin's contributions to the Beach Boys from years ago.

"It gives me a big old chuckle because I wouldn't have thought so forty years ago," said Chaplin on if he believed he would still be singing the song. "I really wouldn't have thought I'd still be talking about how 'Sail On, Sailor' came about. But I guess it's become a classic, and newer fans want to know more things about it. I would have never thought, 'Hey, man, this is going to stand the test of time.' Not at all. It was like, 'OK, I'm going to sing this song, let me try to sing it good and that's it.'

"I don't know if I had been doing it every night for the past forty years if I'd feel that way," said Chaplin. "But now, it's nice and fresh and clean and has a harder edge when we do it live and has a stronger back beat blues thing. I'm quite happy to still be singing it."

Mike Love, left, said that Blondie Chaplin and Rickey Fataar were welcome additions to the Beach Boys in the early 1970s.
(Photo by Mike Morsch)

Discography

The Beach Boys
"Carl and the Passions - So Tough"
and
"Holland"

Released May 15, 1972
Released Jan. 8, 1973

Carl and the Passions - So Tough

Side one
1. You Need a Mess of Help to Stand Alone (3:27)
Brian Wilson/Jack Rieley
2. Here She Comes (5:10) Ricky Fataar/Blondie Chaplin
3. He Come Down (4:41) Al Jardine/B. Wilson/Mike Love
4. Marcella B. (3:54) Wilson/Tandyn Almer/Rieley

Side two
1. Hold On Dear Brother (4:43) Fataar/Chaplin
2. Make It Good (2:36) Dennis Wilson/Daryl Dragon
3. All This Is That (4:00) Jardine/Carl Wilson/Love
4. Cuddle Up D. (5:30) Wilson/Dragon

Holland

Side one
1. Sail On, Sailor (3:19) Brian Wilson, Tandyn Almer,
Ray Kennedy, Jack Rieley, Van Dyke Parks
2. Steamboat (4:33) Dennis Wilson, Jack Rieley
3. California Saga: Big Sur (2:56) Mike Love
4. California Saga: The Beaks of Eagles (3:49) Robinson

Jeffers, Al Jardine, Lynda Jardine
5. California Saga: California (3:21) Al Jardine

Side two

1. The Trader (5:04) Carl Wilson, Jack Rieley
2. Leaving This Town (5:49) Ricky Fataar, Chaplin, Carl Wilson
3. Only with You (2:59) Dennis Wilson, Mike Love
4. Funky Pretty (4:09) Brian Wilson, Mike Love, Jack Rieley

The fiction behind a fine girl and her story

SELF-TITLED
Looking Glass
(1972)

Elliot Lurie picked up his J-200 acoustic guitar and sat down in the upstairs bedroom of a farmhouse that he and his bandmates had rented in Hunterdon County, New Jersey.

The farmhouse had been built around the turn of the 20th century and was surrounded by 88 acres of farmland. The band, which had been fairly successful playing bars and fraternity houses in the late 1960s in New Jersey and Pennsylvania, had rented it for $240 a month with the hopes that it would provide an atmosphere that was conducive to creating music that would take the band to the next level.

Even though he was just out of college in 1970, Lurie had already developed his own style of songwriting, which included playing a chord sequence and melody that worked for him, and then just free associating from there.

In high school, Lurie had a girlfriend named Randye. So he started inserting the name Randye into the lyrics of what he was creating that day in his bedroom.

"I got the story in my head and I had a few lines with a verse that was kind of interesting. Then I got to the chorus and to Randye," said Lurie. "But Randye is a weird name because it can be taken as a male name or a female name."

There was an upright piano in the living room of the

The members of Looking Glass in 1972 included Larry Gonsky, Pieter Sweval, Jeff Grob and Elliot Lurie, far right.
(Photo courtesy of Elliot Lurie)

farmhouse where the band rehearsed. Lurie wrote the chorus and bridge on that piano.

"The chorus and bridge have these triads that remain the same while the bass notes move to change the chords," said Lurie. "That's accomplished better on piano than guitar."

Elliott Lurie wrote and sang lead on "Brandy," which became a No. 1 hit for Looking Glass.
(Photo courtesy of Elliot Lurie)

So as the song evolved, Lurie kept running back and forth between the guitar upstairs and the piano downstairs.

"Finally, I said to myself, what an idiot, take the guitar downstairs. Why do you keep running up and down?" said Lurie.

That problem was solved, but as the song continued to evolve, Lurie was still having trouble with the name of the main character, "Randye."

"The song is about a barmaid, so I thought why don't I change the name to 'Brandy.' So that's what I did," said Lurie. "But when I first finished writing it, I didn't jump up and down and say this is a hit."

But it was. Not only that, but "Brandy," by the band Looking Glass, would go on to become one of the most iconic songs of the 1970s.

There were, however, a series of twists and turns that complicated the efforts to even get the band's recording career off the ground.

Elliot Lurie, keyboardist Larry Gonsky, and bassist Pieter Sweval, were all classmates at Rutgers University in the late 1960s. They were joined by drummer Jeff Grob, who attended a nearby New Jersey community college.

One evening, the four of them were sitting in Lurie's 1965 Chevy convertible — "imbibing something or other," according to Lurie — and trying to think up a name for the band.

"We were looking in the rearview mirror and we thought, what's another way to say mirror? Well, looking glass would be another way. And it was the 1960s and that had some kind of psychedelic overtones," said Lurie. "What we liked about the name was that we were kind of like ordinary guys and we thought we were sort of a reflection of whoever may be listening to us."

Looking Glass made a local name for itself as a cover band, playing local bars and frat houses at Rutgers and Princeton University in New Jersey, and at Lehigh University in Pennsylvania.

As the band became more successful on the local scene, it would mix some original songs into its sets, something that Lurie said was "tolerated" by the local following the band had established.

Upon graduation, the band members each wanted to pursue a career in music, an idea that didn't originally sit too well with their parents.

"Of course, they were all appalled because we were middle class and lower middle-class kids and our parents had saved up to send us to state university in New Jersey, and the idea of becoming musicians was abhorrent to them," said Lurie.

But the band members all convinced their parents to give them a year to see if they could make it in the music industry. And that's how the young musicians ended up in the rural New Jersey farmhouse, creating music and honing their craft during the week, while maintaining their bar and frat house gigs on the weekends.

Although the exact details are lost to history, the band met someone who knew someone in the music industry. And that someone was Mike Gershman, a successful West Coast music publicist who was tired of the publicity business and tired of the West Coast, and had moved back to the East Coast looking for something to do.

Gershman saw Looking Glass play, liked what he heard, and offered to manage the group. Since he had connections in the music industry, the band members agreed to let him be their manager.

The first thing the band did was travel to Saugerties, New York, to record some demo tapes in a studio near where Gershman lived. Those demos would eventually make their way to record executive Clive Davis, then-president of Columbia Records.

Davis, too, liked what he heard, especially "Brandy," and he wanted to hear the band perform live. So he set up a showcase gig for Looking Glass to open for Buddy Guy at the Cafe au Go Go in Manhattan. And based on what Davis saw that evening, he signed Looking Glass to Epic Records, the label that Columbia used for new artists.

Things happened pretty quickly from there. Davis suggested the band travel to Memphis, Tennessee, to record four songs with Steve Cropper at his Trans Maximus Inc. Recording Studios. Cropper had been a guitarist for Booker T. & the M.G.'s in the 1960s and when that band broke up at the beginning of the 1970s, he had produced and played on sessions for Poco, Jeff Beck, Jose Feliciano, Yvonne Elliman and John Prine.

"Steve was a wonderful gentlemen, had a great history and a beautiful studio down there and we cut four sides, including 'Brandy,' with Steve in Memphis. We were quite happy and came back to New York," said Lurie. "Then we had a meeting in Clive's office and listened to what we had recorded in Memphis. And we listened to the four tracks and all of us — Clive and we and Mike Gershman all agreed — that they sounded like nice recordings for a bar band, but that they didn't sound like hits."

It was time to regroup and rethink. Davis next decided to put Looking Glass into the studio with Sandy Linzer, an old-school New York writer/producer who had co-written the Top 10 singles "Let's Hang On" and "Working My Way Back to You" for the Four Seasons.

This time, Linzer came to Looking Glass at its New Jersey farmhouse, where the band had all the necessary recording equipment set up.

"He was extremely helpful. He took the arrangement of 'Brandy' and really helped us mold it. It was a very good session," said Lurie.

But Linzer made one suggestion for the next session that didn't sit well with the band members: He wanted them to sing on the recording but he wanted session musicians to play on the track

The band members said no. Linzer relented, and Looking Glass once again recorded "Brandy," the vocals and the instrumentation, this time at Olmsted Recording Studio in midtown Manhattan.

"I went in and did the vocal overdubs, we did the background vocals, everything. It was great," said Lurie.

But not yet great enough. Linzer wanted to "sweeten" the record by putting horns and strings into the arrangements. He also wanted to put some sound effects at the beginning of the song — the sound of waves and a ship's bell.

"I hate to use the word, but it was kind of schlocky," said Lurie. "It was a schlocky pop string and horn arrangement layered on top. We hated it. And every time they ran it through, we hated it more and more."

The band members decided to take a break from the session and headed up to the roof of the recording studio to have a smoke and ponder what they had just heard.

"We just looked at each other and said, 'We can't live with this. It's just not us,'" said Lurie.

Somehow, and Lurie isn't quite sure how, the band members eventually convinced Davis that although they were happy with what Linzer had done with the music to that point, the situation just wasn't going to work for them. They wanted to produce their first album, the self-titled *Looking Glass,* by themselves.

Davis gave them the green light to proceed on their own. So the band hooked up with Bob Liftin, an engineer who owned Regent Sound Studios in New York. Lurie redid the lead vocals on "Brandy" yet again, and he and Gonsky put together a different horns arrangement to add to the song.

"We really didn't know much about doing the arrangement and when we had it copied, it was all incorrect. So we wound up humming the parts to the horn players. That's expensive, a seven-piece horn section. But we worked them through it," said Lurie. "And finally, before 'Brandy' was released as a single, we even changed it a little bit more in the mastering process. We sped it up just a little bit more just slightly. So when people try to play along with the record, they get very confused because it's halfway between the key of E and F. We sped it up the old-fashioned way, where you turn the tape recorder speed up. It raised the pitch a little bit and raised the tempo a little bit, but it's kind of in-between keys. And that's the finished record that you hear."

The rest of the *Looking Glass* album was done with what Lurie calls "a hunt and peck production system."

"Again, we really didn't know much about what we were doing," said Lurie. "Bob Liftin was a great engineer. But we took too much time on everything and probably paid too much attention to the wrong things and not enough attention to the right things. And we managed to squeak an eight-song album out of it."

Four of the songs on the album were written by, and had lead vocals by, Lurie. The other four songs on the album were written by and had lead vocals by Pieter Sweval.

Once the album was completed, it was released on June 6, 1972. But "Brandy" wasn't the first song to be released as a single. The band members liked a Lurie-penned song, "Don't It Make You Feel Good," as the first single.

"We put it out and it did nothing," said Lurie. "That could have been it right there; that could have been the end of the story."

But it wasn't. As was often the case in those days, Harv Moore, a disc jockey at the Top 40 radio station WPGC-AM/FM in Washington, D.C., was urged by Robert Mandel, a promotions man at the record label, to listen to the "Brandy" track off a test pressing of the LP.

"The promotion man went in to hang out with Harv and he said, 'Have you heard this Looking Glass thing?' And Harv said, 'Yeah, but it's not really happening.' And the promotion man said, 'You really got to listen to the rest of the album; this group is pretty good.' Back in those days, that could happen. A promotion man could have a relationship with a disc jockey and ask him to listen to something and he would," said Lurie.

Moore liked "Brandy" a lot. And he played it a lot. A week later, the band members got a call from record company officials telling them that a disc jockey in Washington, D.C., had put "Brandy" in regular rotation on the station and the phones were ringing off the hook.

"The record company guys said, 'You're gonna have a No. 1 record.' And we said, 'Are you sure?' And they said, 'We've done this before; we do this for a living. If you have a song in a major market like this and the requests are like that, it's going to be a hit.'"

Within a few months, other radio stations in other major markets around the country had “Brandy” in regular rotation and the fan reaction was the same.

Looking Glass had a smash No. 1 hit single.

Suddenly, they needed an agent and had to start booking dates for a tour to support the album.

“It was interesting because with one big hit, you can headline a 500- 600-seat club. But you can’t really make money that way. Back in those days, maybe it was tour support money, but we didn’t get any,” said Lurie. “So we would do those 500- 600-seat clubs and then we would fill it other dates by opening for much bigger acts. It was a very unusual tour because we’d go out to headline a little club and the next night we’d be opening for the Jeff Beck Band or Alice Cooper or Steely Dan. Some of these worked well and some of them not as well. When you’re opening for Alice Cooper where his act involves him chopping his head off with a guillotine and then you come out there singing ‘Brandy, you’re a fine girl,’ it’s not gonna work.”

Laurie recalls one story that helped him maintain his perspective in that whirlwind of being a rock star with a hit record.

On Labor Day weekend of 1972, Looking Glass was booked to play the Steel Pier in Atlantic City, at one time one of the most popular entertainment and amusement parks in the country. But this was at a time when both the Steel Pier and the city were in decline, and before gambling was legalized in New Jersey.

One of the main attractions at the Steel Pier was a diving horse, which was popular from the mid-1880s and had become a permanent attraction at Steel Pier in 1924.

“We stayed at this little motel across the boardwalk from Steel Pier. You had to actually walk the length of the pier to get to where the show was, which was at the end. And the other act performing on the pier was Duke Ellington and his

Orchestra, which was phenomenal," said Lurie. "So the first day we come down to get our gear set up. We spoke to the guy there and asked him when do we go on? We were doing three shows a day. He pointed over to behind the stage and said, 'You see that diving board up there? There's going to be a horse that is going to walk up the stairs to the top of that diving board. And that horse is going to dive into that pool. When you hear that splash, you hit it.' That kind of put it all in perspective."

Despite the success of "Brandy," which made it to No. 1 on the U.S. Billboard Hot 100 Singles charts, the U.S. Cash Box Top 100 Singles chart and the Canadian RMP Singles chart, the *Looking Glass* album only made it to No. 113 on the U.S. Top 200 Albums chart in 1972.

Although the album itself didn't run up the chart, it did attract the attention of another big-name artist — Bob Dylan.

After the album's release and while Looking Glass was preparing to go on tour, the band would rehearse in a downtown Manhattan studio, which also served as a rehearsal studio for other top musicians of that era. And one day, word filtered to the band members that Dylan was also in the studio.

"A little later, into our rehearsal walked Bob Dylan. We took a little break to talk to him. He said he liked 'Brandy' but he said, 'There's one other song on the album that I really like, too, that "Stanton Station" one.' First of all it shocked me that he liked our stuff, but it shocked me that he had actually heard the album and knew 'Stanton Station,'" said Lurie. "Now since that day, I've had a number of contacts with Bob Dylan through people I know who know him. I've learned that he's quite the musicologist and listens to everything. Now it makes sense to me. But the fact that he had heard an album cut off a Looking Glass album was shocking to me at the time."

The strength of "Brandy" enabled the band to get back into the studio in early 1973 to record its second album, *Subway Serenade.* And although Davis had capitulated and allowed Looking Glass to produce its first album, for the second one, he suggested the band work with producer Arif Mardin.

Mardin had started his career at Atlantic Records in 1963 and had risen though the ranks quickly as producer and arranger, working with Petula Clark as well as the Rascals in the late-1960s. At the time, Mardin was working on *Abandoned Luncheonette,* the second studio album by a not-yet famous Daryl Hall and John Oates.

"Arif Mardin is one of the great record producers of all time and one of the most wonderful gentlemen you'd ever want to meet," said Lurie. "Going from producing ourselves and not really knowing what we were doing to working with Arif Mardin at those fabulous historic studios, it was a fantastic experience."

The *Subway Serenade* album would feature the single "Jimmy Loves Mary-Anne," also written by Lurie, and intended as a follow up to "Brandy" with the hopes of once again capturing some magic.

"Jimmy Loves Mary-Anne" was actually written by Lurie while Looking Glass was recording its first album. The band was still living in the farmhouse in New Jersey, but the New York recording sessions sometimes ran into the early morning hours. Lurie's parents still lived in the same Brooklyn apartment complex where he grew up, and Regent Sound Studios was closer to his parents' place in Brooklyn than it was to the Jersey farmhouse.

So on some of these late nights, Lurie and drummer Jeff Grob would crash on couches at Lurie's parents' apartment rather than drive back to rural Jersey.

"It had the old fire escapes on it and it was the summertime. I went out on the fire escape and it just brought back those young teenage memories for me of the kids in Brooklyn, and the Jimmy and Mary-Anne characters were part of that," said Lurie.

"Jimmy Loves Mary-Anne" reached No. 33 on the U.S. Billboard Hot 100 Singles chart, No. 31 on the U.S. Cash Box Top 100 Singles chart, No. 21 on the Canadian RPM Singles chart, and No. 16 on the U.S. Adult Contemporary chart.

However, the *Subway Serenade* album itself would not chart.

And just as quickly as it had started, it was over for Looking Glass. Lurie left the band in 1974 to pursue a solo career and although the band tried to continue on with different members and even different names, by late 1975 everyone had gone their separate ways.

Lurie attributes that to a couple of things.

"One is there was a schizophrenia about the band in that we had two writers, two singers and the direction was not uniform between the two creative forces behind the band. It's not that we didn't get along and that Pieter didn't appreciate my material any more than I didn't appreciate his material. But as a listener, it was like what band is this?" said Lurie.

"The second problem was we were a four-piece garage band — guitar, bass, drums and piano. When we went on the road, we didn't have a horn section. There were no playback tracks then, there were no synthesizers that could emulate horn sections. So when people came to see us and they wanted to hear 'Brandy' the way they heard it on the radio, they heard the same voice and they heard the same rhythm section but they didn't hear the same record. There was no 'there' there. There was 'Brandy' the song, but the band itself was too much all over the map to make the connection."

"It's unbelievable to me that the song has endured the way that it has," says Elliot Lurie. (Photo by Patti Myers)

Lurie said the band realized that by having the big hit on the first album, it had to find a way to have a viable follow-up hit somewhere on the second album.

"Arif Mardin produced 'Jimmy Loves Mary-Anne' and it's a beautifully produced record. If you listen to that record today on vinyl with good speakers, it still sounds great," said Lurie. "And I think 'Jimmy Loves Mary-Anne' was the closest song we had to a hit on the second album. But it just didn't connect the way 'Brandy' did."

As to why "Brandy" resonated with fans in the early 1970s and continues to do so today, Lurie is still astounded.

"It's unbelievable to me that the song has endured the way that it has. I think part of it is the lyrics. People identify with a story song. Another part of it is that hunt-and-peck production of it that we did. When you hear that song on radio today, it doesn't sound quite as dated as some of the other things do because it's not quite a Grass Roots record and it's not quite a rock record. There is something a little different about it," he said.

"And the vocal is interesting because I hadn't sung that much in the studio before I did that vocal. I started singing the vocal the first time and Mike Gershman, the manager, called me in and said, 'You've got to do something about that Brooklyn accent.' So in the vocal, if you notice, all the Rs in the song are really accentuated because a Brooklyn guy who doesn't pronounce his Rs is trying extra hard. So there are all these eccentric things about the record — the production is a little different, the vocal is a little different, the story is a little different. Maybe that's the reason."

As for the stories behind "Brandy" and "Jimmy Loves Mary-Anne," they're the products of creative imagination and writing, according to Lurie.

There was a theory floated in recent years that the inspiration for "Brandy" was actually a woman named Mary Ellis, who had never married and lived in New Brunswick, New Jersey, where Rutgers University is located and where Lurie went to college. Local legend has it that Ellis was seduced by a sea captain who vowed to return from his journeys to marry her. Ellis allegedly would look out over the Raritan River in New Brunswick awaiting his return, which never did happen.

But Ellis wasn't the inspiration for the song, according to Lurie.

"No, that's an incredible coincidence," he said. "I write fiction."

Discography

Looking Glass
Self-titled
Released June 6, 1972

Side one
1. Jenny-Lynne (3:02) P. Sweval
2. Brandy (You're a Fine Girl) (3:17) E. Lurie
3. Catherine Street (5:48) P. Sweval
4. Don't It Make You Feel Good (2:51) E. Lurie

Side two
1. Golden Rainbow (3:05) E. Lurie
2. Dealin' With The Devil (3:18) P. Sweval
3. From Stanton Station (3:48) E. Lurie
4. One By One (6:01) P. Sweval

There's a little bit of "Good Time Charlie" in a lot of us

O'KEEFE

Danny O'Keefe

(1972)

Danny O'Keefe was feeling tied down. He was married, had a child and was working in a restaurant supply business in a small town in Washington state in 1966.

He wanted a more interesting and exciting life.

So O'Keefe bought a Triumph Bonneville motorcycle from a friend and would frequently ride to Seattle and hang out in the scene there. While riding the bike itself may have given O'Keefe some more of the type of life that he craved, it just about killed him, too.

A motorcycle mishap in which he was injured could have delayed his quest to get on a faster track with his life, but the period of recuperation turned out to be fortuitous: It gave him the time to write songs and hone his skills on the guitar.

And ever so slightly, life started to turn in the right direction for O'Keefe and his family.

"We were penniless, but it was an exciting time," said O'Keefe.

One evening, in what O'Keefe calls "probably an encapsulation of all that I'd been going through," a song just kind of flowed out of him.

"From the first time I played the song to Jerry Dennon, with whom I had a publishing and recording contract, I knew it was a strong song. There was a model of sorts for the song in an older friend who had just had a heart attack but was still living fast and hard. But I'm sure there are many people in that song, including myself."

It was called "Good Time Charlie's Got the Blues," and O'Keefe first recorded it in 1967, but didn't release it. Instead, a band called the Bards, from Moses Lake, Washington, recorded the song and released it as the B-side to the song "Tunesmith" on Parrot Records, in 1968. The song didn't attract much notice.

That same year, O'Keefe had joined a psychedelic rock band called Calliope, which recorded one album called *Steamed* for Buddha Records, disbanding shortly thereafter.

"Good Time Charlie's Got the Blues" wouldn't resurface again until 1971, when O'Keefe recorded it for his self-titled debut album. That version also failed to garner any attention.

The following year, he re-recorded the song, this time with a slower, more downbeat arrangement, for his second album, called *O'Keefe.*

And that's the one that hit.

That version of the song was released as a single and reached No. 9 on the Billboard Hot 100 Singles chart; No. 5 on the Billboard Adult Contemporary chart; and No. 63 on the Billboard Hot Country Singles chart.

"Good Time Charlie's Got the Blues" would go on to be covered by numerous artists over the years, including Elvis Presley, Willie Nelson, Waylon Jennings, and Dwight Yoakam. Charlie Rich's cover of the song was on his 1980 album *Once a Drifter*; Leon Russell's version also reached No. 63 on the Billboard Hot Country Singles chart in 1984; and Mel Torme recorded a version of it for an episode of the television series *Night Court* titled "Leon, We Hardly Knew Ye."

"It's always an honor when another artist records one of your songs. Evidently, many people related to the song in their own lives," said O'Keefe. "I hung out with Waylon a bit, and his is my favorite version, other than my own. But we didn't discuss why he cut it. I think it was obvious. He and the others who recorded it found a resonance within their own lives. It's a very simple song and easily relates to a musician's life as well as to the person hearing it. We all think it will be better for us someplace else."

O'Keefe's first album, called *Danny O'Keefe,* was produced by Ahmet Ertegun for Cotillion, a subsidiary label of Atlantic Records, that was formed as an outlet for blues and deep southern soul records. It was recorded in Muscle Shoals, Alabama, and Los Angeles.

"Ahmet was a charismatic presence in the studio, but he probably wasn't truly a producer in the strict sense," said O'Keefe. "He also had many demands on his time. When we were in Muscle Shoals, he was relatively isolated and it was a set group of musicians, so it was easier to concentrate. When we went out to LA to cut tracks, it was more difficult."

But neither O'Keefe nor Ertegun were pleased with the recording of "Good Time Charlie's Got the Blues."

"We didn't get the right version with the first recording," said O'Keefe. "I think the A&R people were convinced that it was a strong single, but had the wrong arrangement."

Because of that, Cotillion decided to release the song "Covered Wagon" as a single, and while it got a little airplay, the song didn't do much.

Ertegun wasn't hired to produce O'Keefe's second album. Instead, Arif Mardin, who had mixed the first recording of "Good Time Charlie's Got the Blues" on the first album, would end up producing O'Keefe's second album, with the strikingly unoriginal title *O'Keefe.*

"We decided to go to Memphis and recut the song and another set of songs," said O'Keefe. "Arif had recorded Dusty Springfield at American Studios in Memphis and had a feel for both the studio and the [session] players. It was a good fit and we were able to successfully record the 'hit.'"

"Arif was a gracious gentleman and we hit it off," said O'Keefe. "We knew the first recording wasn't going to be very successful, but everyone still thought 'Good Time Charlie's Got the Blues' was a hit."

As to why O'Keefe's first two albums had the same titles, he has a simple answer now: "Not too bright, I guess."

Nevertheless, when O'Keefe and Mardin were putting together songs for the 1972 *O'Keefe* album, they enlisted the help of background singers Eddie Brigati and his brother, David Brigati.

Eddie Brigati had already made his mark with the Rascals, co-writing such hits as "A Beautiful Morning," "Groovin'," "People Got to Be Free," "I've Been Lonely Too Long," "You Better Run," and "How Can I Be Sure," with Rascals songwriting partner Felix Cavaliere.

Eddie had left the Rascals in 1970 after the group's contract with Atlantic Records had expired. David Brigati, sometimes known as "the fifth Rascal," was a studio background vocalist for the group but did sing lead on the title track of the Rascals' 1968 album *Once Upon a Dream.* David's involvement with the band ended when Eddie left the Rascals.

The two would record an album in 1976 called *Lost in the Wilderness* under the name Brigati.

Mardin had coproduced the Rascals' *Once Upon a Dream* album and knew the Brigatis, and it was through that connection that the brothers would lend their vocals to the *O'Keefe* album.

"The Brigatis were very tight vocally and were able to think on their feet and come up with vocal ideas. They were also hilarious, so it was great fun to work with them," said O'Keefe. The follow-up single to "Good Time Charlie's Got the Blues" off the *O'Keefe* album was called "The Road." O'Keefe had actually composed the song prior to writing "Good Time Charlie's Got the Blues."

"There was little interest from the people at Atlantic as the album had been released to Signpost Records," said O'Keefe. "The people running Signpost had a falling out with the Atlantic executives and there was very little support for the album or the second single. As I was a leased artist and not directly signed to Signpost, I think they thought we'd just go back in the studio and cut another record with a new single."

Although "The Road" would get lost on the *O'Keefe* album, it would resurface in 1977 when Jackson Browne covered it on his *Running on Empty* album.

"'The Road' was one of those songs that hints at something to come more than the situation at the time and that has proven true," said O'Keefe. "I'm sure there's a Kerouac influence, but I don't know how much I thought about that at the time. In many instances, you're writing from the subconscious and the ideas that float to the top are probably generated from something roiling within that eventually finds words. I still think that's the case in my writing."

O'Keefe was pleased with Browne's version of the song.

"Jackson was going to call the album *The Road and the Sky* and he thought my song 'The Road' fit well into the concept," said O'Keefe. "I loved the concept of recording the album in hotel rooms and on the bus, etc., and I was proud of his version of the song."

Of the songs on *O'Keefe*, the artist would write all of them with the exception of "Honky Tonkin'," a Hank Williams tune.

"I don't know if I could say why I decided to put it on the album other than that I loved the song," said O'Keefe. "I used to think it was interesting to record a song by someone who had been a big influence, and certainly Hank Williams was all that."

As for the album cover, O'Keefe said that "unfortunately," he did have input into the art and design. It's a painting of O'Keefe wearing what appears to be a coonskin cap, leaning against a tree in an outdoorsy, rural mountain setting.

"I loved the Quicksilver Messenger Service's cover for *Happy Trails*, which had been supervised by George Hunter, a former Charlatans band member," said O'Keefe. "We used the same artist — whose name has slipped into the river — and it was painted from a photo George took at my place in Seattle.

"I don't think I had a well-informed idea of what I wanted and the record company had hoped for something better, but we went with it because they wanted the album out," he said. "As an aside, the cap is not coonskin, but red fox, harvested from a Goodwill bin. My wife was a good seamstress and she fashioned the hat for me. I was satirically challenged in those days."

O'Keefe said that in trying to make a mark in the early 1970s music scene, he wasn't particularly aware of what the motivating forces were for him.

"I learned fairly early on in my writing career to not pay too much attention to what my peers were doing," he said. "I didn't listen extensively to any of my contemporaries after I caught myself writing Rolling Stones songs after listening to too much *Beggars Banquet*. It's easy to be seduced, but it's of very little value. Listening to people from different genres is more rewarding and the better ideas come from the language and people you hear around you, as well as from prose and poetry."

The *O'Keefe* album would peak at No. 87 on the Billboard 200 Albums chart based on the strength of "Good Time Charlie's Got the Blues."

But O'Keefe doesn't consider the *O'Keefe* album his best.

"I wouldn't think so, but I have very little perspective on that," he said. "I would think *Breezy Stories* [which would be his next album, released in 1973] is better, but there is much about my later work that I like as well.

"It's difficult, I think, for the artist to make much judgment on his or her work. That's not the job. Following and developing the creative urge is the only thing that really matters in the process of discovery. You hope to be reified by the process, but every new recording project is a roll of the dice. You hope to eventually be successful at being yourself."

Discography

Danny O'Keefe
"O'Keefe"
1972

1. Good Time Charlie's Got The Blues (3:01)
2. Shooting Star (2:38)
3. The Question (Obviously) (3:37)
4. Honky Tonkin' (2:51)
5. The Road (3:48)
6. Grease It (3:16)
7. An American Dream (5:14)
8. Louie The Hook Vs. The Preacher (3:37)
9. The Valentine Pieces (3:16)
10. I'm Sober Now (3:37)
11. Roseland Taxi Dancer (2:45)
12. I Know You Really Love Me (0:59)

The Rat Pack was everything that you could imagine

ANKA

Paul Anka

(1974)

During the times that the two of them had a chance to talk privately, Paul Anka would ask Frank Sinatra what it was like to be back on top of the music industry in the 1970s.

By then, Sinatra had already established himself as a huge singing and film star. Anka had left his mark as well in the late 1950s and early 1960s as a teen idol, writing and singing hit songs like "Diana," "Lonely Boy," "Put Your Head on My Shoulder," and "Puppy Love."

Then in 1964, the Beatles came to the United States. And as the music changed and evolved, so did a lot of American artists — particularly crooners like Sinatra and Anka — for much of the rest of the decade.

In 1968, Anka wrote the lyrics for "My Way," a song that Sinatra would record and release on a 1969 album by the same name. The single reached No. 27 on the U.S. Billboard Hot 100 Singles chart and No. 2 on the Easy Listening chart. In the United Kingdom, "My Way" spent 75 weeks — from April 1969 to September 1971 — in the Top 40, a record for a single in the U.K., and would go on to become Sinatra's signature song.

"Frank had such a soft spot when I'd ask him, in broad terms, if he'd like to have a hit again," said Anka. "And he'd say, 'Man, there's nothing like having a hit record out there.'"

Anka had gotten to hang around with Sinatra and the rest of the Rat Pack — Dean Martin, Sammy Davis, Jr., Peter Lawford, Joey Bishop — in the early 1960s, when those artists virtually owned Las Vegas. They called Anka "The Kid."

"As a nation, you got your information from *The Ed Sullivan Show* and *American Bandstand.* And then you heard about these guys — these stylish, cool guys — not getting into real trouble but just living it. The Rat Pack music was out there. Dean had hits, Frank had hits. And that's all that you heard," said Anka. "Back then, the music and the sense of style was evolving."

And Anka, along with another young crooner of the time, Bobby Darin, were right in the middle of the Vegas scene.

"It was all about these cool guys. And us as young guys, we all wanted to be cool like them. We wanted to dress like them. I wanted to stand in front of a band like them," said Anka. "Oh, it was just amazing. They were the coolest to be around. It was everything that you could imagine."

Anka's longtime friendship with Sinatra, and the success of having written "My Way," put Anka in a position to get back on the charts himself in the 1970s, a decade that was unfolding as a diverse period in music history.

By 1974, it had been more than 10 years since Anka had recorded a Top 25 hit. He switched record labels, from Buddha Records to United Artists, and teamed up with singer Odia Coates to record "(You're) Having My Baby." Written by Anka, the single made it to No. 1 on the U.S. Billboard Hot 100 Singles chart and anchored his album, *Anka,* released in 1974.

And what Sinatra had said about having a hit record resonated once again for Anka.

Paul Anka wrote the lyrics for "My Way," a song that Frank Sinatra would record and release on a 1969 album by the same name. It would go on to become Sinatra's signature song.
(Photo by Mike Morsch)

"It's so true. You're up to date, you're current. The feeling is like you've been rewarded," said Anka. "I was kind of coming off the 'My Way' thing and I was really writing again. So it was gratifying to reach that goal. That was a very, very cool feeling."

From the early 1950s to the mid-1970s, the music business infrastructure included independent record companies that were addressing the necessity of change that had occurred over that period.

"It was pretty much the landscape that these guys [the independents] were as viable as the big labels," said Anka. "Artists went to the independent labels because they had people that believed in you, people that believed you were a priority."

Anka had survived the second half of the 1960s by performing regularly in Las Vegas and in Europe. He was particularly popular in Italy.

At the beginning of the 1970s, he had a couple of minor successes with Buddha Records, including the 1971 self-titled album *Paul Anka,* which featured the single "Do I Love You," that made it to No. 53 on the U.S. Billboard Hot 100 Singles chart; and with the 1972 album *Jubilation*, the title track of which got to No. 65 on the U.S. singles chart.

But Anka believed changing labels would help his career, so he looked at the possibilities and eventually signed with United Artists.

"They believed in me and I was a priority. They got it. And I liked the people and the promotions staff," said Anka. "It was not unusual for me to kind of look at what was on the table from majors to independents. The indies had great rapport with the disc jockeys; they were out there promoting and they could do things the big labels couldn't. But I went where I believed in the people and where the people believed in me."

When it came time to make the *Anka* album, Anka had been keeping an eye on what Rick Hall was doing in Muscle Shoals, Alabama. Hall was a producer, songwriter, music publisher, owner of FAME Studios in Muscle Shoals, and founder of what would become known as the Muscle Shoals Sound.

By the early 1970s, Hall had turned his attention from soul music to mainstream pop music, producing for the Osmonds, Donny Osmond's solo efforts, and Tom Jones.

Anka had written the hit single "She's a Lady" for Jones in 1971.

"I was watching this guy Rick Hall — there was an eclectic array of things that he was doing — but I liked the sound that was coming out of there [Muscle Shoals] and I was looking for that new sound for me," said Anka. "The songs that I was writing . . . the whole feel to me needed to be a lot more natural, to have a personality from somewhere."

So Anka set up a meeting with Hall. And the two clicked.

"He got what I was doing. The feel from the city-type labels and studio work, the younger groove that was down there and the way they recorded, was such a stark difference and it all made sense to me. I didn't want to continue cutting records in New York or cutting records at RCA Studios in LA. I loved what I saw down there and that was the magic."

According to Anka, he wrote "(You're) Having My Baby" for women who wanted children but didn't necessarily want to be involved in a relationship. And he was thinking about recording the song as a duet.

Neil Bogart was an executive at Buddha Records, and while there, Anka had worked with a gospel group called the Edwin Hawkins Singers.

Bogart liked a singer named Odia Coates, who at the time was a member of the Northern California Youth Choir, founded by Edwin Hawkins. Bogart had remained friends with Anka after the label change, and when Bogart found out that Anka was considering doing a duet for the *Anka* album, he recommended Coates.

"I was always looking for new talent. I always had a little opening in my head. When Neil told me about Odia and sent me some music, I got really interested. I flew her down [to Muscle Shoals] and loved her. I said wow, what a great thing it would be to put her on 'Having My Baby' and see what happens," said Anka.

Anka had a sense the song was something special.

"I knew something was happening with 'Having My Baby.' On 'My Way,' I knew it was a home run. You get a sense of what you've got and you get a sense if you've captured this amazing moment," said Anka. "And I knew from the feedback we were getting when we tested 'Having My Baby.' Radio would have never played that song about four years before that. But when radio went, yeah, this is a good song . . . then you know."

Not only did "(You're) Having My Baby" become a No. 1 hit, it also caused a stir in 1974.

According to his 2013 autobiography *My Way*, Anka addressed that controversy.

"It was a song I thought nobody would object to — who could possibly be against that?" wrote Anka. "We were growing up as a country, things were evolving, and obviously the situation of women was changing radically. A whole new wave was starting. Some women's magazines thought it was condescending and hipsters naturally thought it was corny. *Rolling Stone* hated it. The National Organization for Women gave me its 'Keep Her in Her Place' award and *Ms.* magazine called me 'Male Chauvinist Pig of the Year.'

"But there was really no such thing as bad publicity. It generally ends up doing something for you; controversy was always a plus. In the end, I never needed to get up on a soapbox to answer my critics because suddenly everybody was coming to my defense. Even *Time* magazine wrote, 'What are you getting on this guy's case for? We're in a war. We've got a drug plague. We've got shit going on in our country. Give him a break, he's writing a song about his wife.' Overnight, with all the heat, the record went to No. 1. Go figure," Anka wrote.

In addition to "(You're) Having My Baby," Anka and Coates recorded "One Man Woman/One Woman Man" for the *Anka* album. He had written the song on a guitar while in a motel in Muscle Shoals. That single was also a hit, making it to No. 7 on the U.S. Billboard Hot 100 Singles chart and No. 5 on the Billboard Adult Contemporary chart.

The *Anka* album would be Anka's highest charting studio album, reaching No. 9 on the U.S. Billboard 200 Albums chart.

Anka and Coates would work together again after the *Anka* album was released. They recorded "I Don't Like to Sleep Alone," which made it to No. 8 on the singles chart, and "(I Believe) There's Nothing Stronger Than Our Love," which got to No. 15 on the singles chart, both in 1975; and "Make It Up to Me in Love," a sequel to "One Man Woman/One Woman Man" in 1976, although it didn't chart.

"With Odia, she became a whole part of my thing there for a while. And then when I got the news that she had the cancer, I sent her to Boston and all these clinics but I couldn't help her. It was just a very sad loss," said Anka.

Coates died at age 49 in 1991 after a four-year battle with breast cancer.

Now in his mid-70s, Anka has had a song in the Billboard Top 100 during seven consecutive decades. He had recorded more than 125 albums worldwide, and his LP and singles sales collectively have amassed more than $90 billion according to Broadcast Music, Inc., the largest music-rights organization in the U.S.

He still performs regularly and shows no signs of slowing down.

"If you're healthy and you've still got the passion, you can't quit from an industry like this. That really spreads over to anything. I think anyone that still has a passion for something should not ever retire," said Anka. "That's what we're about on that stage, the professionalism, the musicality and the fun in it. If you're not having any fun, to me, philosophically, you've got to sit down and have a little meeting with yourself."

As for the music he made in the 1970s that put him back on the top of the charts, Anka said that if one dreams hard enough, works hard enough and makes wise decisions, an artist can remain relevant.

“If you listen to those records from that period, they had a different thing than anything I’d ever done,” he said.

Discography

Paul Anka

"Anka"

1974

1. **Bring The Wine (4:11)**
2. **One Man Woman / One Woman Man (3:45)**
3. **Something About You (2:50)**
4. **(You're) Having My Baby (2:32)**
5. **Let Me Get To Know You (2:52)**
6. **Love Is A Lonely Song (3:56)**
7. **How Can Anything Be Beautiful (After You) (2:37)**
8. **I Gave A Little And Lost A Lot (3:02)**
9. **Papa (3:38)**
10. **It Doesn't Matter Anymore (3:38)**

"Jeez, you sound just like the radio"

WHO LOVES YOU

Frankie Valli and the Four Seasons (1975)

In the mid-1960s when he was 11 years old, Lee Shapiro was watching the *Ed Sullivan Show* with his mother on a black-and-white TV, when Frankie Valli and the Four Seasons made their appearance on-screen.

"Look, this band doesn't have just guitars. There's a guy playing acoustic piano," Shapiro recalled telling his mother. "I could do that. Maybe someday I could be in a band like that."

The guy playing acoustic piano for the Four Seasons was Bob Gaudio, who wrote the group's first No. 1 single, "Sherry" in 1962, and followed that by co-writing with Bob Crewe a string of hits including "Big Girls Don't Cry," "Walk Like a Man," and "Rag Doll."

Eight years later, in the mid-1970s, Shapiro was studying music composition at the Manhattan School of Music and also playing keyboards and doing arrangements for an 18-piece jazz band in a club in New Jersey. One evening at the club, the road manager for the Four Seasons approached Shapiro and told him that the band was looking for a keyboardist who was also an arranger, to replace Gaudio.

"The guy says, 'Bob Gaudio is leaving and whenever the band wants to do a new song, Charlie Calello arranges. But he's not traveling and he doesn't play keyboards. So can you do that?' And I said, 'Sure, I can do that,'" said Shapiro.

Lee Shapiro was offered the gig to be one of the "new" Four Seasons in 1973 at the age of 19 while still a student at Manhattan School of Music.
(Photo by Mike Morsch)

"A couple of days later, the bass player [for the Four Seasons], Joe Long, called me and offered me a chance to audition, which happened to be in an Italian restaurant and banquet hall because the band was financially in hock at that point," said Shapiro.

"I went in and auditioned and Frankie Valli walked into the room. I put the music to 'Dawn (Go Away)' in front of me," said Shapiro. "I put my hands down and played the chord and Frankie sang, 'Pretty as a midsummer's morn, they call her Dawn,' and I stopped playing. Frankie looked at me and said, 'What's the matter?' And I said, 'Jeez, you sound just like the radio,'" said Shapiro.

Despite that star-struck moment in 1973, Shapiro was offered the gig to be one of the "new" Four Seasons at the age of 19 while still in school. But he wasn't sure whether to accept the offer, and went back to the Manhattan School of Music looking for advice.

"I went to my composition professor, who was an eighty year old woman, and I said, 'I just got an offer to play keyboards and tour as one of the Four Seasons.' And her answer was, 'Lee, I don't know who the Four Seasons are, but if you're telling me they're going to pay you to play piano, orchestrate, tour, and record, I think you should do it,'" said Shapiro. "And with no effort and not concentrating on or chasing it or pursuing it in any way, I replaced Bob Gaudio and become the piano player in that band."

Shapiro was familiar with music of the Four Seasons but admits he wasn't particularly a fan. He appreciated what Frankie Valli and the Four Seasons had created and accomplished, but he was more into the Beatles, the Beach Boys, and some of the Motown artists at the time.

Although he was just 19 at the time he joined the Four Seasons, Shapiro had already been recording for a couple of years, so he wasn't a stranger to the studio work. The first project he did with the Four Seasons was a group of five songs.

"Bob Crewe, the original producer, was involved. The songs got released, but they didn't become hits because that happens," said Shapiro.

Even though the Four Seasons were regrouping in the mid-1970s, Valli had started to regain some standing as a solo artist. He hadn't had a hit in several years when he recorded a solo album called *Closeup* that was released in February 1975. That album included the single "Swearin' to God," written by Crewe and Denny Randell, that reached No. 6 on the U.S. Billboard Hot 100 Singles chart.

Since he was one of the "new" Four Seasons, Shapiro was invited by Calello to the recording session for "Swearin' to God."

"I went there and Charlie was there and they were recording the saxophone solo on top of the record. And I said, 'Hey Charlie, what do you want me to do?' And he gave me the best advice that anyone has ever given me in a studio. He said, 'Lee, I'd like you to go sit over there in the corner, keep your mouth shut, and listen to what goes on all day.' And let me tell you something — no one can learn more than what I learned in that one day," said Shapiro. "He obviously had confidence in my ability to absorb what was going on and take it in. Discussion was not part of the day. It was observance and learning. And it happened for me and I was forever changed at that point. I got the jones. I wanted to make recorded music, I wanted to produce, I wanted to do that."

But first things first. The now-reconfigured Four Seasons had their first album to make.

The group next recorded a song in 1975, written by Gaudio and his future wife, Judy Parker, called "Who Loves You," which had to be made on spec. Even though they were the Four Seasons, they hadn't made an album for three years and they didn't yet have another record deal. Not only that, but the band had to ask for a distribution deal from Warner Brothers.

Fortunately, the head of A&R (artists and repertoire) at Warner's thought "Who Loves You" was, in Shapiro's words, "amazing."

"Honestly, I thought it was just kind of basic chords, just like the oldies were, that had been given a dance treatment. I had no idea how to go about making a hit record because I never had. I knew how to make music. So if something sounded like it was a hit, it was likely that it sounded like it was already on the radio," said Shapiro. "It wasn't until it was completely recorded and mixed and I listened to the playback with everybody that I said, 'Wow, this thing sounds good. It may be on the radio.' And it was."

It would be the title track of the first album for the Four Seasons with the "new" lineup: Shapiro on keyboards, John Paiva on guitar, Don Ciccone on bass, and Gerry Polci on drums. Polci and Ciccone would share lead vocals with Valli. Gaudio would produce the *Who Loves You* album, and Long, who had left the band by this time, would back the group on bass and vocals.

There were actually three versions of the song "Who Loves You" recorded and released in the United States. The version on the *Who Loves You* album begins with a short percussion section before the start of the vocals and clocks in at four minutes and 20 seconds. The single's A-side starts with a fade-in beginning, starting with the first word of the lyrics and is 4:04 long. And the B-side of the single, called "Who Loves You (disco version)," is a shorter version that features two instrumental breaks.

The "Who Loves You" single was released in August 1975 and spent 20 weeks on the U.S. Billboard Hot 100 Singles chart, which was longer than any previous single by the Four Seasons. It peaked at No. 3 on the chart.

The album itself, recorded at the Sound Factory in Hollywood, California, was released in November 1975. But the "Who Loves You" single wouldn't be the biggest song on the album.

A month after the album's release, a second single, "December 1963 (Oh, What a Night)" was released and it shot right up to No. 1.

According to Shapiro, the song wasn't originally called "December 1963," it was called "December 1933." It was another song written by Gaudio and Parker — they wrote all eight tracks on the album and featured Polci on lead vocals, Ciccone, who had been the lead singer for the Critters — singing falsetto, and Valli singing lead on the bridge sections, and background on the rest of the song.

"The song was about prohibition. And we went to Gaudio and we said, look man, we love this song but we really hate the lyrics," said Shapiro. "And he flipped out. At the time, he was thirty-two years old and had written a bazillion hits already and we were nobody; we were his band."

But according to Shapiro, Gaudio recognized the fact that the "new" Four Seasons were 10 to 12 years his junior, and that they might have a point.

"And he changed it and we went back in and recorded it and ended up having the biggest-selling hit in the history of the franchise," said Shapiro.

There was one other song from the album called "Silver Star" that was released as a single in early 1976 that made it to No. 38 on the U.S. Billboard Hot 100 Singles chart.

Despite the strength of three Top 40 singles, two of which were Top 5 hits including a No. 1, the *Who Loves You* album peaked at No. 38 on the U.S. Billboard 200 Albums chart.

With all that was happening in the mid-1970s, and with disco dominating for a few years in the middle of the decade, Frankie Valli and the Four Seasons were relevant and thriving again.

"We had a whole second career with Frankie in the 1970s," said Shapiro, who remained with the Four Seasons into the early 1980s before going on to arrange and produce for several artists, including Frank Sinatra, Barbra Streisand, Barry Manilow, and Chaka Khan. "It was surreal. I started out playing in clubs because the Four Seasons were a has-been band in 1973. But I still loved being part of it because it was the biggest damned thing that I had ever done. It was unbelievable."

Shapiro considers himself fortunate to have grown up in the 1970s era of music and to participate at a time in the music industry where songs were still the driving force in music.

"Today, the driving force in music, which I love also, is basically audio production. If you listen to a song now, it's pretty much about the sonic effect coming off the record and the sound of the bass drum and the riffing and samples that are used and the instrumentation of the synthesizers. Again, it's masterfully created, but it has nothing to do with words and lyrics, melody and lyrics," he said.

That's why Shapiro believes that *Jersey Boys*, the longtime smash Broadway hit production that first opened in 2005, chronicling the music and lives of Frankie Valli and the Four Seasons, has had such success.

"*Jersey Boys* made such an easy transition into Broadway because it's all so damn sing-able and memorable. Also, it was basically for the baby boomers; it was the soundtrack of their lives," said Shapiro. "I knew it would be a huge hit for the same reasons that Frankie Valli's music and Frankie Valli's voice and Frankie Valli as an entity had huge hits in the 1960s and then again in the 1970s."

Although *Jersey Boys* doesn't directly feature much about the "new" Four Seasons, it does include songs in the show that Valli and the Four Seasons did in the 1970s, including "Who Loves You," "Oh, What a Night" and "Fallen Angel," all songs that Shapiro arranged in the 1970s.

"People say you weren't in *Jersey Boys*, doesn't that make you mad? I say, folks, no Frankie Valli, no nothing. I'm thrilled that they saw my talent and valued it enough to make me part of it," said Shapiro.

Right in the middle of the success of *Jersey Boys*, Shapiro approached Valli, Gaudio and Calello with the idea of putting together a group called The Hit Men, guys who had served as members of other bands through the years, such as Elton John, Paul McCartney, Carole King, Carly

Simon, Jim Croce, Rod Stewart, Cheap Trick, and Blood, Sweat and Tears.

"I told them I was thinking of putting this together," said Shapiro. "I said I know there are a lot of guys out there doing tributes, but being that I was one of the Four Seasons, what do you think?

"Frankie said, 'I have no restrictions. Go and do it. You were one of the Four Seasons, you can play the songs.' He was supportive," said Shapiro.

In November 2010, Shapiro did indeed put together The Hit Men, which, as of 2017, included lead guitarist/vocalist Jimmy Ryan, bassist/vocalist Jeff Ganz, keyboardist, percussionist, and vocalist Russ Velazquez, and drummer and vocalist, Steve Murphy. The band is not a tribute act, nor are the musicians former cast members of the Broadway musical. They are the actual artists who helped rocket so many songs to the top of the Billboard charts.

But Shapiro doesn't forget where he started.

"It was a fabulous, fabulous, most important event in my life to become one of the Four Seasons. I'm grateful for the whole thing and I hope what I provided helped them perpetuate the success, and apparently it did," he said.

Discography

Frankie Valli and The Four Seasons
“Who Loves You”
November 1975

All songs written by Bob Gaudio and Judy Parker
1. Silver Star (6:05)
2. Storybook Lovers (3:43)
3. Harmony, Perfect Harmony (4:46)
4. Who Loves You (4:22)
5. Mystic Mister Sam (4:23)
6. December, 1963 (Oh, What a Night) (3:36)
7. Slip Away (3:04)
8. Emily's (Salle de Danse) (6:40)

The big hit that he didn't want to record

TRYIN' TO GET THE FEELING

Barry Manilow

(1975)

In the early 1970s, Barry Manilow had established himself by producing two successful albums with the three hit singles, "Could It Be Magic," "Mandy," and "It's a Miracle." He was starting to be taken seriously as an artist and was beginning to carefully craft his image.

When it came time to look for songs for his third album, *Tryin' to Get the Feeling,* Manilow and co-producer Ron Dante were inundated with possibilities. Both were songwriters and producers, and had decided the third album would contain a mix: half the songs would be written or co-written and arranged by Manilow and the other half would be songs written by other artists.

"We had an abundance of riches in those years. Everybody was throwing songs at us. Every good songwriter in the world was trying to get their songs to me so I could get Barry to listen so we could consider them for the next album," said Dante.

Among those pitching songs to the duo was Arista Records founder and president, Clive Davis. He had a song called "I Write the Songs," written by Bruce Johnston of the Beach Boys, that he thought would be perfect for Manilow.

But Manilow didn't like the song.

Ron Dante had first met Barry Manilow in the early 1970s when both were singing jingles in commercials. Dante would go on to produce many of Manilow's albums in the 1970s. (Photo by Mike Morsch)

"Clive funneled it to Barry and me and he said, 'Listen to David Cassidy's version or the Captain and Tennille's version. This might be a good song for Barry,'" recalled Dante. "And Barry said, 'The critics are going to kill me. I didn't write the song. I'm a songwriter, and the first words out of their mouths are going to be, "Barry's big hit record that he didn't write is called 'I Write the Songs.'" 'I can't do this song.'"

According to Davis in his memoir, *The Soundtrack of My Life,* he had already suggested "Tryin' to Get the Feeling" to Manilow, which the singer had started to perform in his live shows to a positive reaction from audiences, prior to recording it.

"Then I inadvertently put my finger right on the sore spot of our relationship," Davis wrote. "The next track I played for him was 'I Write the Songs.' Perhaps my enthusiasm over finding the song, which I was certain would be a massive hit for him, had blinded me to how he would respond to it. To say the absolute least, his response was not positive."

Bruce Johnston, who had left the Beach Boys in the mid-1970s for a solo career, wrote "I Write the Songs," which would become one of Barry Manilow's signature songs. (Photo by Mike Morsch)

Johnston had joined the Beach Boys in 1965 as a touring replacement for Brian Wilson, who had decided to devote more time to songwriting and producing for the band. By 1972, Johnston had left the Beach Boys for a solo career, and it was during that time he wrote, "I Write the Songs."

There is a belief that he wrote the song for Wilson, but according to Johnston, that's not true.

"I wrote the song for me," said Johnston. "It's a hymn to God for being the person who starts it all. 'I've been alive forever, and I wrote the very first song.' And it gets me nuts when people say Bruce Johnston wrote that song for Brian Wilson. I just thought it was a cool song."

Manilow remained unconvinced, at least on the surface.

"He bluntly told me that he couldn't possibly record that song," Davis wrote in his memoir. "The suggestion truly offended him. Everything about it was a problem. He said that it made him sound like as if he were on a monumental ego trip."

But Davis persisted.

"I could hear the arrangement in my head, and I knew that he could do a killer job with it," wrote Davis. "Once he put his stamp on the song, it wouldn't matter who wrote it. It would be his because he would be the one making the song believable for everyone who heard it. But he wasn't having any of this. I believe Barry genuinely felt that I had insulted him. He stormed out of my office and I didn't hear from him for two or three months."

It took some additional persuading by Dante for Manilow to consider it further.

"I said we can do a great arrangement on this, something that hasn't been done with the other arrangements," said Dante. "I said, it's perfect, we'll put it in the sweet spot of your voice and we'll even put a little homage to the Beatles in the middle of it with the piccolo and trumpet. We loved the Beatles, both of us."

Then one day, Davis got a call from Manilow and Dante.

"He had to see me," wrote Davis. "And when he played his demo of the song for me, it was magic, everything I had hoped for. To his complete credit, Barry came up with a brilliant arrangement. Deep down, he's always been a total pro."

Manilow had relented. And the result was that "I Write the Songs" would be the first single from the *Tryin' to Get the Feeling* album, released in October 1975 by Arista Records, and it was a smash hit. It reached No. 1 on the U.S. Billboard Hot 100 Singles chart in January 1976, after spending two weeks atop the Billboard Adult Contemporary chart in December 1975. It won a Grammy Award for Song of the Year, and was nominated for Record of the Year in 1977.

The album itself was the highest-charting album at that point in Manilow's career, reaching No. 5 on the U.S. Billboard 200 Albums chart. And it further cemented the partnership between Manilow and Dante of co-producing albums.

The two had first met in the early 1970s when both were singing jingles in commercials. Dante had experienced some success of his own in the late 1960s as the lead singer of the contrived group, the Archies, which was a Saturday morning television cartoon based on the comic book characters.

Dante's voice is the lead on the No. 1 single "Sugar, Sugar" by the Archies, but because the song was sung by an animated group, Dante didn't have to tour in support of the single or the ensuing album, *Everything Archie,* that was released in 1969.

"At the time, I was singing in commercials. I was a jingles singer. I was singing for Coke, Pepsi, Doctor Pepper, Budweiser, you name it," said Dante. "My career in jingles took off; it went crazy. They thought, well, we've got the voice of a number one record. So I would get calls from Pepsi, Coke, and Doctor Pepper by the jingles writers asking if I would sing on their commercials. I was having a grand time and I was very happy that it was a hit."

It was on one of those commercial gigs that Dante met Manilow, who was also writing and singing jingles for commercials for many of the same companies.

"I remember meeting him and we were going to sing the commercial together with two other singers, Melissa Manchester and Valerie Simpson. We had a helluva vocal group for that one," said Dante. "It was for a test product for Pepsi. So we sang the spot and it didn't sell."

But Manilow and Dante hit it off.

"Barry said, 'Would you like to listen to some of my songs? I'm working with Bette Midler, but I really want to be the artist, not the arranger and producer. Could you produce for me?'"

Dante agreed, and the two collaborated and co-produced Manilow's first two albums, *Barry Manilow I,* which was released in 1973, and *Barry Manilow II,* released in 1974. When it came time to make *Tryin' to Get the Feeling,* the duo was on a roll.

"We would listen to a bunch of songs, then we'd meet somewhere, usually just before the summer started. And we'd just go through the stuff," said Dante. "First of all, we'd listen to Barry's songs because we had a thing: We would do five or six Manilow songs on each record, but then we'd choose five or six outside songs. The outside songs had to be very special, good for Barry's voice and for his image. He was singing love songs."

In addition to "I Write the Songs" and the title track, the album would feature "Bandstand Boogie," written by Manilow, Charles Albertine, Larry Elgart, Les Elgart, Bob Horn, and Bruce Sussman, that would put words into the theme song for Dick Clark's *American Bandstand* television show.

"That was kind of my idea for him to put lyrics to the Dick Clark theme," said Dante. "I had known Dick Clark for a long time; I had toured with him as a kid. I always said, 'Gee, if somebody would put lyrics to this, Dick would play it every day.' And sure enough, it became the theme song of the show every day for like ten years. It was good publicity and it was a great record to play on."

According to Dante, that's how the two chose the songs for the album, those that would keep Manilow's image intact on each album.

"We tried to move ahead with him in terms of lyrics and melodies on each album," said Dante. "We didn't have a crystal ball, but both Barry and I were musicians first. He plays piano and I play guitar, and we're both singers and songwriters. So we know a good song when we hear it. Especially if it's something good for Barry Manilow. That was the most important thing in choosing the songs."

In addition to the singles "I Write the Songs," "Tryin' to Get the Feeling," and "Bandstand Boogie," the album also featured the song "She's a Star," a nod from Manilow to Bette Midler.

"I always thought that it was a connection to Bette Midler. He would not have written that if he had not worked with one of the greatest stars of that decade," said Dante. "He said she was like the Statue of Liberty. 'She gets out there and is bigger than life.' And he loves her. He always regretted leaving her as her accompanist and arranger. But he had to. Fate had to take them both in their own directions. I think that had a lot to do with that song."

By their third album together, Dante said he and Manilow had developed a formula that was working for them. They had their engineer, they had their studio, and they had their musicians who would come in and put strings and horns on songs.

"We had the group together and it was a great feeling to know that with what we were working on, it had better be good," said Dante. "Because a lot of people were listening and either loving it or criticizing it. So we always tried to top the one before it.

"And that's a credit to Barry. His emotional leanings on a lot of those songs won the world over. We felt really good about our work. It was a labor of love. We wanted to make something that would last through the ages. God was good to us."

The collaboration between Manilow and Dante would continue. The two would co-produce Manilow albums through the rest of the 1970s, many of which would be Top 10 albums, and produce many more hit singles, including the No. 1 hits, “Looks Like We Made It,” “Can’t Smile Without You,” and “Copacabana,” all of which would cement Manilow's reputation as one of the biggest stars of the 1970s and beyond.

“It was the golden age of songwriting, arranging and singing. The songwriting was really strong. You look at the Top Twenty of each year and you’ll see songs that you can hum and even your kids can hum because they’re used in movies, TV, and commercials constantly. They can’t get enough of these classic songs,” said Dante. “The songs were good, the singers were really good; they didn’t need auto-tuning. There were really cool live arrangements; they weren’t computer-generated. There was something really golden about that period of time when those songs were written and sung with heart. People remember them.”

Dante said the songs endure because people want them to endure.

“They want to remember the first girlfriend they had or first boyfriend they had. And nothing triggers a memory like a song. You hear a certain song, you remember the girlfriend, you remember the car, you remember the Saturday night that you were at the roller rink or something,” he said.

“I am constantly grateful to have walked through all of that, to have seen it from the inside out and to have remembered all of it.”

At first, Barry Manilow didn't want to record "I Write the Songs" for his third album, *Tryin' to Get the Feeling.* (Photo by Mike Morsch)

Discography

Barry Manilow
"Tryin' to Get the Feeling"
October 1, 1975

Side one
1. **New York City Rhythm (4:42) Barry Manilow, Marty Panzer**
2. **Tryin' to Get the Feeling Again (3:51) David Pomeranz**
3. **Why Don't We Live Together (2:54) Phil Galdston, Peter Thom**
4. **Bandstand Boogie (2:49) Charles Albertine, Larry Elgart, Les Elgart, Bob Horn, Barry Manilow, Bruce Sussman**
5. **You're Leaving Too Soon (3:30) Barry Manilow, Enoch Anderson**
6. **She's a Star (4:16) Barry Manilow, Enoch Anderson**

Side two
1. **I Write the Songs (3:51) Bruce Johnston**
2. **As Sure as I'm Standin' Here (4:50) Adrienne Anderson, Barry Manilow**
3. **A Nice Boy Like Me (3:58) Barry Manilow, Enoch Anderson**
4. **Lay Me Down (4:20) Larry Weiss**
5. **Beautiful Music (4:32) Barry Manilow, Marty Panzer**

Ordering "Afternoon Delight" right off the menu

SELF-TITLED

Starland Vocal Band

(1975)

It was the first day of the recording session and the Starland Vocal Band was at A&R Studios in New York City, ready to start work on its first album for John Denver's new Colorado-based record label, Windsong Records.

Phil Ramone, who had signed on to be assistant producer and recording engineer for the record, had just finished producing Paul Simon's album *Still Crazy After All These Years*, which would soon be released in October 1975.

"So you want to hear the new Simon and Garfunkel record?" Ramone asked the members of the Starland Vocal Band — Bill Danoff, his wife Taffy Nivert, Margot Chapman, and a then 18-year-old Jon Carroll.

"And we went . . . what?" said Carroll. "And Phil said, 'Well, one of them anyway. I just got the test pressing for Paul's new record. He's on his way over now and I was going to give it to him. But I want to listen to it. Do you want to hear it?'" Carroll recalled Ramone saying to the group. So they sat there in the studio and listened to the first side of *Still Crazy After All These Years*, the second cut of which is "My Little Town," a song that Simon wrote and offered to Garfunkel to use on his solo album, *Breakaway*, which was also being released in October 1975. Despite it being used on solo albums by Simon and Garfunkel, "My Little Town" was the first new single by Simon and Garfunkel since the duo had recorded the 1972 hit "America." "My Little Town," which made it to No. 1 on the U.S. Billboard Adult Contemporary chart and No. 9 on the U.S. Billboard Hot 100 Singles chart, would be perceived by the public — incorrectly, as it turned out — as a reunion of the partnership between Simon and Garfunkel.

Simon finally showed up at the studio while Ramone and the members of the Starland Vocal Band were listening to his new album.

"As I recall, Paul was a little miffed that Phil burned one of the plays of a test pressing for someone other than him," said Carroll. "I have a slight recollection, though, that Phil had a second virgin copy that he gave to Paul."

It wouldn't be the last interaction between Simon, Ramone, and the Starland Vocal Band that week. Danoff had always loved Simon's song "American Tune," from the 1973 album *There Goes Rhymin' Simon,* and wanted to include it on the first Starland Vocal Band album.

Ramone agreed. He had an a cappella arrangement of the song that he wanted the band to record that week and he wanted Simon in the control booth while it was being cut.

"The recording of it really doesn't do it justice. We used to do it during shows and when we did it live, it was pretty spellbinding," said Carroll. "So we stood there right in front of him in the control room and sang it top to bottom and when we finished recording it, Paul had this wide-eyed poker face on. He looked at us and said, 'You know, I've always liked that song. It's always been one of my favorite songs that I've written and I've always thought of it as my song. But from now on, I'll think of it as your song.' That was a nice thing to say. I thought he was very, very gracious," said Carroll.

Paul Simon really liked the Starland Vocal Band's a cappella version of his song "American Tune" when he heard it recorded in the studio. (Photo by Phil McAuliffe)

The Starland Vocal Band recorded its debut album of the same name in two weeks, actually taking three weeks on the calendar in the fall of 1975, with a week off in between recording sessions.

"The thing about working at A&R with Phil Ramone that I was most impressed with was that it sounded so good," said Carroll of the sonic environment there. "Because Phil Ramone really was an engineer first and a musician second. I remember thinking while I was singing, 'Oh, this is wonderful. The reverb sounds perfect; everything sounds just perfect.'"

But the first single released off the album wasn't Simon's "American Tune." No, the first single would become a mega-hit, one written by Danoff, that would go on to be remembered as one of the most iconic songs of the 1970s: "Afternoon Delight."

According to Danoff's website, Nivert credited the song's creation to "a culinary repast."

"Bill wrote this after having lunch at Clyde's in Washington, D.C.," she explained. "It seems Clyde's has a menu called 'Afternoon Delight' with stuff like spiced shrimp and hot Brie with almonds. So Bill ate it — the food that is — and went home and explained to me what 'Afternoon Delight' *should* be.

"Danoff acknowledged that audiences might find hidden meanings in the song. 'I didn't want to write an all-out sex song,' he told Dennis Hunt of the *Los Angeles Times.* 'I just wanted to write something that was fun and hinted at sex. It was one of those songs that you could really have a good time writing.'

"The Danoffs thought they might have had a problem getting airplay for 'Afternoon Delight,' but few stations found it objectionable. 'If the song had been banned, it would have been a real injustice,' Bill said in the *Times.* 'The lyrics are subtle and sophisticated and not at all raunchy. It might have been banned years ago, but not today," according to the Danoff website.

But once the album was done and "Afternoon Delight" was released as its first single in January 1976, it was several months before the song hit big. And it helped that it got an assist from John Denver.

Denver was quite familiar with Bill Danoff and Taffy Nivert. They had written "Take Me Home, Country Roads," which had become the first charting single for Denver as a solo artist. The song got to No. 2 on the U.S. Billboard Hot 100 Singles chart in 1971.

By 1976, Denver's star was huge, and he was about to embark on a big tour of the U.S. called "An Evening with John Denver." He had put together a crack band that included Wrecking Crew drummer Hal Blaine, Steve Weisberg, John Sommers, and Dick Kniss, who had been the bass player for Peter, Paul and Mary. Milt Okun, who had produced many of the Peter, Paul and Mary albums, was friends with Denver from Denver's days with the Chad Mitchell Trio in the late 1960s. It was Okun who had taken Denver's song "Leaving on a Jet Plane" to Peter, Paul and Mary, which the trio turned into a No. 1 hit in 1969.

Okun was also the producer for the *Starland Vocal Band* album and was instrumental in getting the band onto Denver's Windsong Records label.

"So we mentioned to Milt that it would really be great if we could go on tour with John. It would kind of make sense because we were on his label," said Carroll.

According to the story that Carroll was told at the time, Okun did approach Denver about including the Starland Vocal Band on his tour. Initially, though, Denver balked, or more likely, Denver's production company wasn't interested, Carroll believes.

"I think Milt eventually got the brush-off from Denver's people," said Carroll. "But Bill asked Milt to politely ask

John himself."

According Carroll, the conversation between Okun and Denver, as it was told to him then, went like this:

Denver: "Well, Milt, the tour plans are kind of already underway. I've been working for a long time to get to this point in my career where I can do 'An Evening With' and do two acts and an intermission."

Okun: "I know."

Denver: "Do you think being on this tour would be the difference between having a hit single off the album for the Starland Vocal Band?"

"Okun: "Yes, I do."

Denver: "Great. Done. Do it."

"That's the story as I heard it. Later on I realized that these were the people [Bill and Taffy] who wrote the first hit song John ever had and sang with him on records. We were on his label. Of course he was going to put us on his tour. He shouldn't have had to think twice about it," said Carroll.

So the Starland Vocal Band opened for Denver on tour, and got its music exposed to Denver's audience.

"It's still a great thing to do if you can manage it, opening on a major tour because you go on for forty minutes and it's a bulletproof forty minutes. By the time you do the second or third show, you pretty well know what's working and what's not working," said Carroll.

According to Carroll, though, there was still another element to the equation that helped the album and the single shoot to the top: promotion.

"The real aces in the hole were these two guys, Larry Douglas and Jerry Doughman," said Carroll. "We got a call from them about a week or so before the tour, saying, 'We're your promotion guys here at this new label, but nobody is telling us shit. We're supposed to be working for you guys and for Windsong. If we were to come along with you to some of the major markets on this tour, would you guys be willing to visit some radio stations and maybe do some meet-and-greets to help get the product [the album] into stores?' And we said, shit yeah," said Carroll.

The combination of the provocative single "Afternoon Delight" being exposed to the Denver fans on the tour and the extra work the band members put into promoting the album on radio stations and in-store meet-and-greets paid off. And big.

By July 1976, the Starland Vocal Band had the No. 1 hit single in the country.

"There's something about 'Afternoon Delight,' the wry aspect of it, the sort of the wink that the kids maybe will get, maybe they won't. It wasn't naive. And it was musically sophisticated, something that I didn't realize until people started pointing it out," said Carroll. "I gotta say, also, there are certain songs that as soon as you sing it, and you sing it multiple times and people get it and enjoy it. And as you're singing it, you know they're going to get it. It's also musical enough and fun enough to sing it where you never get tired of singing that song."

The *Starland Vocal Band* album reached No. 20 on the U.S. Billboard 200 Albums chart with "Afternoon Delight" reaching No. 1 in both the U.S. and Canada. The album's follow-up single, "California Day," peaked at No. 66 on the U.S. Billboard Hot 100 Singles chart and No. 22 on the Canadian Adult Contemporary chart.

In addition to having a No. 1 single, the band also was nominated for four Grammy Awards in 1977: Best New Artist, Record of the Year, Best Pop Performance by a Duo or Group with Vocals, and Best Arrangement for Voices (duo, group or chorus), and won two, for Best New Artist and Best Arrangement. The song itself garnered Danoff another nomination for Best Song.

Carroll believes that "Afternoon Delight" has managed to stay remarkable rather than being merely just another pop record.

"There are a lot of pop records that are just curious or curiously bad. Now I'm not saying I don't empathize with people who say, 'Jesus, who in the world would listen to that?' And I know who those people are because they're not listening to soft rock; they're listening to hard rock or jazz or R&B. That's me, too. I like all kinds of records. But I know why that record is a hit record," said Carroll. "I had high school chums meet me crossing the street the year following the release of 'Afternoon Delight' being a hit and apologizing to me for throwing paint brushes at the radio during their summer jobs painting houses because the song was played so much on the radio. It was one of those songs people loved to hate."

The Starland Vocal Band would make four more albums through 1980, but none would reach the success of their first. The band broke up in 1981 and Danoff and Nivert divorced shortly after that.

Carroll and Margot Chapman had married while members of the Starland Vocal Band, but later divorced as well. Their son, Ben Carroll, is also a musician.

Jon Carroll has continued as a performer, composer, arranger, producer, songwriter, and musician, and his works have appeared in films and commercials. His songs have been covered by Linda Rondstadt, Tom Jones, and Kenny Rogers. He is still a highly sought studio session performer and is the longtime keyboardist/vocalist with Grammy Award-winning singer/songwriter Mary Chapin Carpenter.

But being a part of the Starland Vocal Band remains a fond experience for Carroll.

"I wasn't as charmed by 'Afternoon Delight' the way the rest of the world was, for no other reason than I was a kid just out of high school and I wanted to rock and roll," said

Carroll. "But I loved the singing. I loved working it out for the song. We really explored all these wonderful combinations of the singers in the group. I really enjoyed that.

"But it puts you in a funny position to have the biggest hit record that you'll more than likely ever have as an artist — and that iconic thing happens — and it happened to be the first thing you did out of the gate and whatever you do after that is going to be the asterisk. That's somewhat of a challenge," he said. "But then you realize it was a great thing and you were lucky to be a part of it. The first group is the first group that you were in. The first group that I was in happened to be with folks who had been doing it for a while already.

"And every generation has been reintroduced to 'Afternoon Delight.' It was a perfect recipe. It's managed to be there that way. I'm proud to have been a part of it."

Discography

Starland Vocal Band

Self-titled

Released 1976

1. **Boulder to Birmingham (4:14) Bill Danoff / Emmylou Harris**
2. **Baby, You Look Good on Me Tonight (3:06)nBill Danoff**
3. **American True (3:24) Paul Simon**
4. **Starland (3:04) Bill Danoff**
5. **California Day (3:35) Bill Danoff**
6. **War Surplus Baby (4:21) Bill Danoff**
7. **Starting All Over Again (3:10) Bill Danoff**
8. **Afternoon Delight (3:13) Bill Danoff**
9. **Hail! Hail! Rock and Roll! (2:44) Bill Danoff / Taffy Danoff**
10. **Ain't It the Fall (3:39) Bill Danoff**

"On and On" makes Bob Marley's wife go off

CARELESS
Stephen Bishop
(1976)

Not long after his debut album *Careless* was released in 1976, Stephen Bishop found himself cornered at a party by Rita Marley, wife of Jamaican singer-songwriter Bob Marley.

She wasn't particularly happy with the lyrics on one of Bishop's songs and she was prepared to give him an earful about it.

The album featured two Top 25 hit singles: "On and On," which peaked at No. 11 on the U.S. Billboard Hot 100 Singles chart, No. 5 on the Cashbox Top 100 Singles chart, and No. 2 on the U.S. Billboard Hot Adult Contemporary Tracks chart; and "Save It for a Rainy Day," which made it to No. 22 on the Billboard Hot 100 Singles chart.

It was the opening verse to "On and On" that had Rita Marley miffed, particularly the first few lines:

Down in Jamaica
They got lots of pretty women
Steal your money
Then they break your heart

"She said to me, 'Oh, you wrote that song. What do you know about Jamaican women? They do not steal your money and break your heart.' She was upset with me," said Bishop. "So I said, 'Well, it was poetic license.' And she said, 'No . .

Stephen Bishop found himself cornered at a party by Rita Marley, wife of the late Bob Marley, because she took issue with the lyrics to one of his songs.
(Photo by Mike Morsch)

. no.' So I pretty much stayed out of sight for the rest of the party."

Admittedly, Bishop didn't actually have any personal insights into Jamaican women at the time, particularly whether they would steal your money or break your heart. "On and On" was written on a routine trip by Bishop to the grocery store in Silver Lake, a residential neighborhood in the central region of Los Angeles.

"One day when I went down to the country store, I came up with the title," said Bishop. "I had wanted to be somewhere else and my landlady had all these flowers from different parts of the world at the house, and it kind of gave me the impression that I was somewhere else. So 'Down in Jamaica . . .' was the first line I sang in the song."

Bishop also didn't have any idea that the song would be released as a single from the album, let alone that it would become a hit. In fact, singer-songwriter Kenny Rankin, a colleague of Bishop's who had developed a considerable following in the 1970s through a steady stream of albums, recorded "On and On" and released it at the same time that Bishop's version was released.

"He got mad at me because my version became a hit and it killed his version. He didn't like it. But we became really good friends after that," said Bishop.

The *Careless* album took a while to come to fruition and included a series of events, all of which were good fortune for Bishop.

Roy Halee, a longtime producer for Simon & Garfunkel, worked for ABC Records. In the mid-1970s, Halee was the head of A&R (artists and repertoire), the division of the label responsible for scouting and overseeing artistic development of recording artists and songwriters.

Halee had met with Bishop — who played live for Halee at that first meeting — and the label executive signed Bishop to ABC Records.

Once signed, Bishop had an opportunity to meet Art Garfunkel. They were introduced by Bishop's friend, singer Leah Kunkel, wife of session drummer Russ Kunkel, who was working on Garfunkel's 1975 solo album *Breakaway* for Columbia Records. Bishop had given Leah Kunkel a cassette tape of some songs that Bishop had written. Leah gave the tape to her husband and suggested he give it to Garfunkel, who was still looking for songs for the *Breakaway* album.

"Art called Leah and they set up a time. I came into the studio during the recording of his *Breakaway* album. He was actually singing 'Disney Girls' when I walked in the studio," said Bishop. "Another songwriter, Craig Doerge, was there, too. He sang a couple of songs for Art, and I sang a couple of songs for Art."

Garfunkel was impressed with Bishop's songs, and chose two for the *Breakaway* album: "Looking for the Right One," and "The Same Old Tears on a New Background."

Art Garfunkel had chosen two of Stephen Bishop's songs for Garfunkel's 1975 solo album "Breakaway." And he asked Bishop to sing backing vocals on he album. When it came time for Bishop to record "Careless," Garfunkel returned the favor by providing background vocals on two songs for the album. (Photo by Mike Morsch)

One of the singles released from *Breakaway* was Garfunkel's cover of "I Only Have Eyes For You," which had been a hit for the Flamingos in 1959. Not only did Garfunkel put Bishop's "Looking for the Right One" on the B-side of "I Only Have Eyes For You," but he also asked Bishop to sing background on it.

After he contributed on *Breakaway,* it was time for Bishop to get started on his own album. But he sputtered a bit out of the gate.

"I went in the studio with Roy Halee producing and he didn't like my piano player that I was using. He wanted me to use his piano player and I wanted to use mine. And we came to a parting of the ways," said Bishop. "I wound up going to work with Henry Lewy [as co-producer]. He was a big engineer who worked primarily with Joni Mitchell, which was really great for me. I thought that was just terrific."

Bishop had a lot of songs that he had already written that were going to be recorded for the *Careless* album. So when he met with Lewy and played him the songs that he wanted to record, Lewy liked him and the project was ready to go.

Careless would actually feature some big-name contributing artists, starting with Garfunkel, who decided to return the favor and provided backing vocals for two songs, "Every Minute" and "Rock and Roll Slave" on the album.

Although neither of those songs would be released as singles off the album, "Save It for a Rainy Day," the second single released after "On and On," would also feature some big names.

If Bishop was caught off-guard at the success of "On and On," he was more confident that "Save It for a Rainy Day" would make the charts.

"I wanted to write a hit. I had this song that I was working on that was real 'hit-ly.' I got my good buddy Jeff Jones to play bass on it and he played this kind of boom-boom-boom-boom-boom for the chorus and it had this kind of radio-ish sound. Russ Kunkel played drums on it," said Bishop. "And I got Chaka Khan to sing on it and then Eric Clapton played the solo on it."

Knowing the right people who knew the right people worked in Bishop's favor this time around. He had met Khan through Richard Holland, a friend who was dating Khan. And it was Bishop's manager, Bob Ellis, who paved the way to meeting Clapton. Ellis was also managing Rolling Stones guitarist Ronnie Wood at the time, and Wood and Clapton were tight.

"Bob said to Eric, 'You'd really like this artist Stephen Bishop; he's really funny,'" said Bishop.

That was enough to get Clapton to Shangri-La Recording Studios in Malibu, built and designed in the early 1970s specifically for Bob Dylan and The Band. That's where Clapton was recording his *No Reason to Cry* album and that's where he would record his contributions to "Save It for a Rainy Day" for Bishop.

"So Clapton and the incredible Pattie Boyd dropped by the studio," said Bishop. "I was like 'Whoa, it's Eric Clapton. Wow.' To tell you the truth, I was even more amazed at her because she had been married to a Beatle and I was a Beatle-aholic at the time. Clapton was a little inebriated at the time, but he wound up doing the solo there."

There was supposed to be a third single released from the album, either "Little Italy" or "One More Night," according to Bishop, but that never got as far as the decision-making stage. ABC Records was starting to disintegrate and decisions like that were left on the table, particularly because the album already had two hit singles and it was time for both the label and Bishop to move on to other projects. The label would be defunct by 1979.

Based on the strength of its two hit singles, *Careless* reached No. 34 on the Billboard 200 Albums chart.

"Up until then, I had tried for six years to make an album. So I was just throwing something against the wall and see if it stuck," said Bishop.

ABC Records was surprised by the album's success. Initially, it printed only 3,000 copies, according to Bishop. When those sold out immediately, the company printed more copies and the records kept selling out.

The album especially resonated on college campuses, according to Bishop, because young lovers liked it.

"People loved to do the wild thing to that album. They thought it was very romantic. But in those days of vinyl, they had to get up and flip the side over," said Bishop.

The attraction that *Careless* had on college campuses following its release in 1976 provided a nice lead-in for Bishop in 1977, when filming began for *National Lampoon's Animal House*. The film, directed by John Landis, is about a group of misfit fraternity guys who challenge the authority of the fictional Faber College administrators. It starred John Belushi, Tim Matheson, John Vernon, Vera Bloom, Karen Allen, Thomas Hulce, Donald Sutherland, and a young Kevin Bacon, appearing in his first film.

Bishop was friends with Landis, and the director cast Bishop in the movie as "Charming Guy with Guitar," a small role that would become quite memorable.

In the film, Belushi plays the character John "Bluto" Blutarsky, a drunken degenerate in his seventh year of college and the sergeant-at-arms of the rowdy Delta House fraternity.

There is a scene in the film where Delta House is hosting an out-of-control toga party. In the scene, "Charming Guy with Guitar" is sitting on the inside steps of the Delta House strumming a guitar, while a group of co-eds dressed in togas look dreamily at him.

The Belushi character is walking down the steps when "Charming Guy" starts singing . . . "I gave my love a cherry, that had no stone. I gave my love a chicken, that had no bones. I gave my love a story, that had no end. I gave . . ."

At that point, the Belushi character grabs the guitar from "Charming Guy" and smashes it against the wall, destroying it.

"I didn't write it. It's a very old fairy tale. People in college would always sing that song. I decided that it would be a good song to do. It seemed like the right song to do in the scene," said Bishop. "The film's producers wanted a song that they wouldn't have to pay money on."

The song is called "The Riddle Song," a 15th-century English folk song commonly used as a lullaby in that era.

The scene took two takes and two guitars were used.

"I have one of the guitars that was smashed and I had everybody in the cast sign it," said Bishop. "Belushi was a funny guy. It was fun to hang out with him. Of course, *Saturday Night Live* was huge then. It was all new and exciting. Usually when things are like that, it's fun."

Bishop did contribute two original songs for the film: "Dream Girl," which is playing on the car radio in the background while the characters Greg Marmalard and Mandy Pepperidge, played by James Daughton and Mary Louise Weller respectively, are on a date; and the theme, also called "Animal House," played over the closing credits, and on which Bishop sang in falsetto.

His work on the film enabled Bishop to meet Karen Allen, who appeared as "Katy," the girlfriend of Donald "Boon" Schoenstein, played by Peter Riegert. Bishop and Allen would be married for a short time in the early 1980s.

As for the *Careless* album, it will always be a special one for Bishop.

"I'm proud of it, but I'm proud of all my little album children. I have nine of them," said Bishop. "When you do creative adventures, like when you make an album, you usually don't anticipate that it's going to be a hit. And if you do think it's going to be an amazing success, usually it doesn't turn out right."

Discography

Stephen Bishop

“Careless”

Released 1976

All songs written by Stephen Bishop.

1. On and On (3:03)
2. Never Letting Go (3:48)
3. Careless (3:45)
4. Sinking in an Ocean of Tears (3:08)
5. Madge (4:03)
6. Every Minute (3:58)
7. Little Italy (3:27)
8. One More Night (4:02)
9. guitar interlude (0:35)
10. Save It for a Rainy Day (3:12)
11. Rock and Roll Slave (3:38)
12. The Same Old Tears on a New Background (2:40)

OUR PLEASURE TO SERVE YOU

The Stanky Brown Group
(1976)

It was a huge weekend for Stanky Brown. The band had been touring California and the Pacific Northwest and had returned to New Jersey on a Friday.

That evening, they lip-synced their current single, "Falling Fast," on the TV show *Live from the Soap Factory.* On Saturday, the band did several radio interviews during the day and then at night headlined two shows at the Bottom Line, a popular club in Greenwich Village, where they were introduced by comedian Robert Klein.

And then on Sunday, the band was the opener for the first-ever concert held at Giants Stadium in East Rutherford, New Jersey, that included Pablo Cruise, and the Steve Miller Band, and was headlined by the Beach Boys. According to a review of the show by Robert Palmer in the *New York Times* dated June 27, 1978, "It was the first rock concert at the stadium, but probably will not be the last. The crowd was well behaved, the facility was run as smoothly and efficiently as one could expect, and the weather was perfect."

The story, however, doesn't include anything about the performances by Pablo Cruise or Stanky Brown because, according to Palmer, "It [the show] started somewhat ahead of schedule, so that the reviewer, still recovering from a very late Newport Jazz Festival concert, missed Pablo Cruise and Stanky Brown."

No matter that the *New York Times* reviewer missed the first two bands. Stanky Brown guitarist Jeffrey Leynor vividly remembers standing on that stage in that environment at Giants Stadium.

"There must have been 70,000 people there," said Leynor. "The stage was probably 100 feet up. It was the largest show I had ever done. I walked out onto that stage and my peripheral vision was filled with humanity."

Leynor said the band got a very good reaction from the crowd.

"It was like anything else; the adrenalin starts to flow. You feel like jumping out of your skin. Then once you start, you're OK and you get in the groove," said Leynor. "The crowd was definitely ready to party. They were hitting beach balls up to us and throwing Frisbees to us and we were throwing them back.

"But seeing that many people in one place like that was incredible. That was probably the biggest weekend we had ever had," he said.

Indeed, it was. And it might have been the pinnacle for Stanky Brown. Unfortunately, the Giants Stadium gig was about as big-time as the band would get.

Stanky Brown got its start in the early 1970s. Rhythm guitarist Leynor, keyboardist James "Jimmy" Brown, and bass player Richard Bunkiewicz all went to Columbia High School in Maplewood, New Jersey, graduating in 1971. They were joined by drummer Jerry Cordasco, who graduated from Seton Hall Prep in nearby South Orange, New Jersey.

Brown and Cordasco were in a band called The Factory, a folk group with a nine-piece horn section. Brown would soon leave The Factory and strike out on his own.

One evening on his way to play a gig in Asbury Park, New Jersey, Brown decided that he couldn't bill himself as "James Brown." There was an already established star — the Godfather of Soul — named James Brown.

The lesser known Brown was a fan of *The Abbott and Costello Show*, a television series that starred the comedy team of Bud Abbott and Lou Costello, and ran from 1952 to 1954. The duo had already established itself as radio and film stars and was looking to make a mark in the infancy of television.

One of the characters on the sitcom was "Stinky," a little boy dressed in a Little Lord Fauntleroy suit, played by an adult actor, Joe Besser, who would go on in the late 1950s to star as the wimpy member of the Three Stooges.

Brown was also a fan of the character Spanky from the *Our Gang* series — also known as *The Little Rascals* — a series that began in 1922 of comedy short films about a group of poor neighborhood children.

So he took the "Stinky" character and combined it with the "Spanky" character and came up with the name "Stanky," which evolved into the Stanky Brown Group.

One of the first things Brown did when he decided to put together a new version of the band, was to go hear Leynor play in a folk group.

"So at the gig, Jimmy liked my stuff and we started playing," said Leynor. "It was just the electric bass and regular piano with the guitar."

The band — which now included Brown, Leynor, Bunkiewicz, and Cordasco — first attracted the attention of John Scher, who promoted shows at the Capitol Theatre in Passaic, New Jersey, and later at the Meadowlands and festival sites all over America. Scher put the Stanky Brown Group onstage for its first show at the Capitol Theatre on February 9, 1973. The band was supposed to open for Melanie Safka — known as Melanie — who was only one of three women to perform at Woodstock, and who in 1972 had a No. 1 hit with "Brand New Key."

But according to Leynor, Melanie had suffered a miscarriage and was unable to perform. So to replace her,

Scher brought in multi-instrumentalist singer-songwriter David Bromberg and the comedian Robert Klein.

From there, the band continued to attract attention, this time from the newly formed Arista Records, founded in 1974 by record producer Clive Davis, who had been the president of Columbia Records from 1967 to 1973 before striking out on his own.

But according to Leynor, Davis wasn't hearing what he wanted to hear from the band.

"Clive said, 'I love the songs that you guys write, but I don't hear a hit song,'" recalled Leynor.

Arista did, however, press a song by the band called "Rock 'n' Rollin' Star," but it went nowhere.

"It wasn't written by us and we hated it," said Leynor. "We played it like garbage every time we had to play it live. Nothing like cutting your nose off to spite your face."

During that time, the band did hook up with Jim Mason, who had co-produced *A Good Feelin' to Know,* the fourth studio album recorded by Poco and released in 1972. Stanky Brown did a bunch of demos with Mason producing to present to Davis, but again, nothing impressed Davis.

Eventually, Arista's interest faded, and Stanky Brown signed with Sire Records, and that's where things started to happen for the band. They would make three albums for Sire: *Our Pleasure to Serve You* in 1976; *If the Lights Don't Get You the Helots Will* in 1977; and *Stanky Brown* in 1978.

Our Pleasure to Serve You was recorded at 914 Sound Studios in Blauvelt, New York, the same studio where Bruce Springsteen had recorded *Greetings from Asbury Park* in 1972.

The recording sessions for *Our Pleasure to Serve You* were "like dying and going to heaven," according to Leynor.

"It was my first professional album. There were a lot of insane nights, driving up the Garden State Parkway to the studio," said Leynor. "We had some interesting people play on that album."

Among those was Eric Weissberg, best known at the time for playing banjo on "Dueling Banjos," the theme song for the movie *Deliverance,* which was released as a single and reached No. 1 on the U.S. Billboard Easy Listening chart in 1973.

Also in the studio for the album was Leslie West, founding member of the hard-rock band Mountain. He had recorded with The Who during the band's 1971 *Who's Next* New York sessions.

"Leslie West came in to do lead guitar because I'm a writer and a singer and rhythm guitarist; I don't play lead," said Leynor. "I was out there in the studio all by myself with him, and of course it was like standing next to the Empire State Building. The guy came in and ate five pizzas, shot heroin, and then blew my teeth out with his guitar work. Those days were nuts."

For its first album, the Stanky Brown Group was implementing all the influences of its band members.

"We thought we were going to be the next Beatles. Jimmy and I, even though we were very different, we were pop-influenced. Everybody that we worked with said it's [a song] got to be two-and-a-half minutes, it's gotta be the kind of thing that you would start humming. So that's who we were taught by and that's really who we listened to, AM radio," said Leynor. "So we mixed folk and rock together. And also a little country thing like Poco. So all of those things were there in the music. But it eventually changed as we toured more, because there was a need for more live lead guitar and horns."

Our Pleasure to Serve You sold more than 100,000 copies, according to Leynor. The most recognizable song from the album is "You've Come Over Me," he said.

The closest the band came to "making it," Leynor said, was with its second album *If the Lights Don't Get You the Helots Will*. That album included the song "Coaltown," which Leynor had written, and ended up on one of the K-tel International compilation albums that K-tel marketed "as seen on TV."

"That song started to break out on AM radio stations in the south and in West Virginia, where the coal mining industry was big," said Leynor. "But somehow Sire messed that up and that was it."

As it happened, 1978 — the year the band played the Giants Stadium gig — was the turning point for the group.

It had one last turn in the spotlight in May 1978 opening for the Blues Brothers — John Belushi and Dan Aykroyd — the first time they played to a live audience outside of their *Saturday Night Live* appearances. The event was a "Bill Bradley for Senate" benefit concert at Rutgers University in New Brunswick, New Jersey.

"The place went nuts. Everybody was there that night — Bill Murray, Gilda Radner, Garrett Morris," said Leynor, rattling off the stars of *Saturday Night Live* from that era. "Belushi was out of his mind coked up, but Danny Aykroyd was so wonderful. That was hysterical fun."

But band breakup was quickly approaching.

"Disco was really big and the first music videos were coming out," said Leynor. "We got dropped by Sire. And that marked the death knell for us."

The group eventually disbanded and Leynor left the music business, attended Jewish Theological Seminary, and became a rabbi. He now works in Texas with hospice patients and with Texas law enforcement, focusing on homicide, suicide, and domestic violence cases.

Stanky Brown did reunite briefly in 2008 and went into the studio to record a reunion album.

"I had been pestering Brown that while we're all still alive, let's just come together one more time. Jimmy wanted to do something I wrote a long time ago that never made it on a record. He said we were just gonna put songs on this record that we like," said Leynor. "It was put out by us, there was no fanfare, no nothing. It actually got a little airplay in Jersey and a few other places. But it was interesting because I had not been in a studio and I had not worked like that in more than thirty years."

Despite having had recording opportunities in the mid- to late-1970s and opening for a number of big-name bands, Stanky Brown never did get to the next level of stardom.

"We were good enough, but we were not star material. I think it was the kind of thing that we wrote some songs that if other people did, they could have become hits," said Leynor. "If somebody had taken us under their wing, had us dress right and put together a live show, it might have been different. I think it was probably one of the most creative periods in all of rock and roll. Stanky Brown wrote some really good songs and we were pretty tight. We didn't get booed off the stage. But it wasn't meant to be."

Discography

The Stanky Brown Group
"Our Pleasure to Serve You"
Released 1976

1. Masquerade (3:26)
2. You've Come Over Me (3:52)
3. Let's Get To Livin' (3:29)
4. U B U (2:30)
5. A Hundred Times Around (5:16)
6. Don't You Refuse (2:44)
7. Friday Night Without You (2:50)
8. Matthew (3:01)
9. Misery Loves Company (3:07)
10. Ravin' Beauty (3:27)
11. Where Have They Gone (3:47)

A real record made by a fictional character

TONITE! AT THE CAPRI LOUNGE
LORETTA HAGGERS
Mary Kay Place
(1976)

It was early 1976 and the television series *Mary Hartman, Mary Hartman* had become a smash hit in syndication.

The series, a satirical soap opera produced by Norman Lear and featuring Louise Lasser in the lead role, took place in the fictional town of Fernwood, Ohio.

It was a hectic time for the show's actors. They were shooting 35 pages of script a day, five days a week for the show that followed its main character through complex life events that reflected a changing social fabric in 1970s America.

One of the show's breakout characters — Loretta Haggers — was Mary Hartman's best friend and neighbor. Loretta, played by Mary Kay Place, was a wannabe country singer on the show. And it helped the character tremendously that Place, who would win a Primetime Emmy Award for Outstanding Actress in a Comedy Series in 1977 for her role as Loretta, could actually sing.

But something unexpected happened. The success of the fictional show and fictional Country and Western singing character Loretta Haggers attracted the attention of real record labels.

They wanted Loretta Haggers to make a country album.

"There was so much work [on the show] to be done I couldn't even think about making an album," said Place. "But I was also afraid that it might be a novelty record and I really wasn't interested in making a novelty record."

The first label to approach Place's agent about making a Loretta Haggers album was Scepter Records' owner, Florence Greenberg. Greenberg had formed her first label, Tiara Records, in 1958, and the first song recorded and released for the company was "I Met Him on a Sunday" by the Shirelles. She then sold the company and the Shirelles contract to Decca Records, and with that money formed Scepter, one of the leading independent record labels of that era. By 1976, Greenberg had produced several stars, including Dionne Warwick, Tammi Terrell, and B.J. Thomas.

"But I didn't have any information other than they just wanted to make a record. And I really didn't have time to go to New York and discuss it," said Place.

It was a call from Emmylou Harris and Canadian record producer Brian Ahern that eventually changed everything for Place and made a Loretta Haggers album a reality.

Harris was coming off a big debut album in 1975, produced by Ahern, whom she eventually married, called *Pieces of the Sky*. It was released by Reprise Records, whose parent company was Warner Brothers Records. The album contained covers of "For No One" by the Beatles; "Tonight the Bottle Let Me Down" by Merle Haggard; and "Bluebird Wine," written by a young Texas songwriter, Rodney Crowell.

Harris had also put together what was called the Hot Band, which included guitarist James Burton and pianist Glen Hardin, both of whom had played with Elvis Presley. Burton had also played in Ricky Nelson's band in the 1950s

Willie Nelson recorded a duet with Mary Kay Place, called "Something to Brag About," that reached No. 9 on the U.S. Billboard Country singles chart. (Photo by Phil McAuliffe)

and Hardin had been a member of the Crickets after the death of Buddy Holly.

Aside from Crowell, other members of the Hot Band included drummer John Ware, pedal-steel guitarist Hank DeVito, and bassist Emory Gordy, Jr.

Harris, Ahern, and members of the Hot Band were all fans of *Mary Hartman, Mary Hartman*, and all wanted to make a record with Place as Loretta Haggers.

"They wanted to make a real record," said Place. "I was a big fan of Emmylou Harris and I knew what an artist she was. She was the real deal. It wasn't a joke."

Place was presented with the full package: Harris would contribute, Ahern would produce, and the Hot Band would back Loretta Haggers. With all that in order, Place chose to accept an offer from Columbia Records as the label.

"I had an incredible band of musicians, plus Emmy was ascending rapidly in the music industry. She and Willie Nelson were right in the thick of what was happening in country music at the time," said Place. "So it was the perfect opportunity. But it was a terrifying opportunity because I really didn't have the experience of singing live in front of people. I just sang in my own bedroom.

"I decided that years later, when I was in the rest home with my teeth in a glass next to the bed, that I would be really annoyed with myself, no matter how frightening it was, to not take advantage of this extraordinary opportunity. I wouldn't have done if it hadn't been for Emmy and Brian and the band. I knew I had the integrity of their work to guide me. So I jumped into this pool — it was the ocean really — feet first. And it was the most fun that I've ever had in my life," said Place.

The album would be called *Tonite! At the Capri Lounge Loretta Haggers,* and would be recorded at an old house in Coldwater Canyon in the Santa Monica Mountains of Los Angeles. Crowell was then living in a Silver Bullet

Airstream trailer on the grounds. Ahern had brought in a big truck with all the recording and producing equipment and had run big cables into the house. The drums were set up in the living room, and in other sections of the house, baffles and banks of guitars were set up. The vocal area was baffled off by another wall.

"Because there was a lot of land around the house, we didn't have to worry about making noise. It was absolutely stunning and beautiful, surrounded by nature," said Place. "We'd often work all night long. We'd get there around four or five pm and work sometimes until three or four am. I could never have done this while I was shooting the show. There was no way. I had a break, and that's when I did that album."

But that wasn't all. Other big names started to drop by and contribute to the album, including Mickey Raphael, the harmonica player for Willie Nelson's band. Linda Rondstadt also stopped by, and so did Dolly Parton, both to lend backing vocals on some of the songs.

"The thing was, obviously the Loretta character was the reason I got the album. And even though there were songs that had a sense of humor or a tone like Loretta might have, I tried to sing as best I could. If Loretta didn't sing on pitch or something was off or there was some kind of mistake on the show, it didn't matter because she wasn't really a professional. But on this record, I made every attempt to do the best vocal work I could do. That's the difference between me and Loretta," said Place.

"I did have Loretta's accent. I did sing with a southern accent. But the challenge was to just make a good record that worked not only as Loretta, but one that anyone would want to listen to, as opposed to a novelty record that wasn't very satisfying musically."

Place had two writing credits on the album: "Vitamin L," which was the first track on the record, and "Baby Boy," both of which she would eventually sing on episodes of *Mary Hartman, Mary Hartman*.

Parton would write one song for the album, "All I Can Do," on which she would sing backing vocals. Parton also sang backup on two other songs on the album, "Good Old Country Baptizin'," and "Coke and Chips."

This was happening when Parton was not only one of the hottest country stars, but was making the transition into being a crossover artist. Additionally, she was in the midst of having her own television variety show, *Dolly*, which ran in 1976 and 1977.

"Dolly could not have been sweeter or more fun. I was singing her song, but it was extraordinarily generous of her to participate. She knew Brian and that's how it happened, because he had asked her to participate," said Place.

There has been much speculation that the Loretta character was based on Parton, and Place thinks that may have had something to do with a writer for *Mary Hartman, Mary Hartman* named Daniel Gregory Browne. He had been one of the contributing writers on the Loretta character for the show.

But Place recalls the creation and development of the character differently.

"I've heard in so many reports that Loretta is Dolly, but I did not base the character on Dolly. I certainly knew her records, but I didn't know Dolly well enough; I hadn't seen her much in person."

Place said she based the character on a combination of a lot of people she knew growing up in Texas.

"I've also read in many articles over the years that Loretta's character is attributed to many different country artists. So it wasn't just Dolly. She has such a specific, unique personality. I'd say maybe my hair might have been based on Dolly."

Tonite! At the Capri Lounge Loretta Haggers took about a month to record, which was about all the time Place had during a break in the shooting schedule of *Mary Hartman, Mary Hartman.*

Upon its release in 1976, the album did well both critically and on the charts. It made it to No. 6 on the U.S. Billboard Country chart. The single "Baby Boy" hit No. 3 in the U.S., while "Vitamin L" cracked the Top 100 Country Singles chart at No. 71.

"I was shocked. It was really exciting for me. It was like a fantasy come true to have a real record. And to get to play with that quality of musicians and singers was daunting and scary and terrifying in many ways. But at the same time, absolutely thrilling," said Place.

And Place believes the album may have surprised a lot of people.

"A lot of musicians were fans of *Mary Hartman, Mary Hartman,* so I think for them it was fun to be on the record because they all watched the show. And it made them laugh. They were happy to participate," she said.

Although Place did occasional concerts here and there, she did not do a full-blown tour in support of the album.

Tonite! At the Capri Lounge Loretta Haggers was the first of a three-album deal that Place had made with Columbia Records. The second album, *Aimin' to Please*, was recorded and released in 1977. It featured the single "Something to Brag About," a duet with Willie Nelson that reached No. 9 on the U.S. Billboard Country Singles chart. And it was that song that helped Place secure a gig hosting *Saturday Night Live*.

Because Place had been a writer on the television shows *M*A*S*H, All in the Family,* and *The Mary Tyler Moore Show* before her acting success on *Mary Hartman, Mary Hartman*, *Saturday Night Live* producer Lorne Michaels had asked her to be a writer on the show. But that was at the time she had accepted the Loretta role on *Mary Hartman, Mary Hartman*, so she declined the offer. She stayed in touch with Michaels and her success as Loretta secured her the *SNL* hosting gig in 1977.

Special musical guest for that show would be Willie Nelson.

Saturday Night Live was going strong and featured its classic lineup of John Belushi, Dan Aykroyd, Chevy Chase, Jane Curtain, Garrett Morris, Bill Murray, Laraine Newman, and Gilda Radner.

"It was crazy, crazy, crazy. They were up all night, every night. That first week I would go out — not as late as they would go out, but pretty late — every night just to get on the night schedule. I'd be awake at eleven pm on a Saturday night. Just shifting your work schedule to the nighttime as opposed to a morning schedule," said Place.

"The boys kind of tested me, John [Belushi] tested me. They kind of tortured me a little bit. And then on Friday they announced that I had passed the test and that there would be no further torture. They just liked to rib you and push you to the limit, see how far they could go. Having an older and a younger brother, I was used to that. There was a lot of teasing and carrying on.

"But they couldn't have been nicer. It was super fun, but it was exhausting because we were burning the candle at all ends of the day and night," said Place.

Her duet with Nelson on the show, for the song "Something to Brag About," went off without a hitch.

"Willie was just in a Country crowd back then, with Waylon [Jennings] and the outlaw thing. That was very trendy then. But he melded and blended beautifully together with the *SNL* cast.

"Willie is an equal-opportunity guy. He likes everybody. He's definitely been that hip for a long time."

Place makes no secret that her role as Loretta on *Mary Hartman, Mary Hartman* changed her life, and it led directly to her success as a real Country and Western artist. Even if it was for a just a short period in her career.

"I love singing. I love recording. The thought of being on the road for long periods of time had less appeal to me, though. It's a very tough life. If, like Emmylou, you've done it since you were a young person, you understand the art of being on the road," said Place. "I'm on the road all the time as an actor and it's still not as rigorous as going from one town to another every day or every other day and singing. It's just really hard. Acting is hard, writing is hard. But there are certain choices. I could not do everything and do any of them well."

Place said she would have had to quit acting and devote her full energies to being a successful country singing artist.

She chose not to. The decision was aided by the fact that Columbia Records dropped Place — and many other artists — after the release of her second album.

Place went on to achieve more success as an actress, starring in dozens of films, including the likes of *Private Benjamin, The Big Chill,* and *The Rainmaker*; and in numerous television series, including *Thirtysomething, Chicago Hope, The West Wing, Law and Order: Special Victims Unit,* and *Grey's Anatomy*.

"I had so many musician friends and I knew what the stress of being on the road was all about and how much energy would be required. And I frankly didn't have that at that point. It was not any choice in a healthy way that I could make," said Place.

"I wanted to be really good at it and I had a lot of work to do to be that good at it. I love music, I love singing; it's still one of the greatest joys of my life. But I'm totally comfortable with the choice I made."

Discography

Mary Kay Place
Loretta Haggers
"Tonight! At the Capri Lounge"
Released 1976

A1. Vitamin L (2:23) Mary Kay Place
A2. Streets Of This Town (Ode To Fernwood) (2:57) Paul Grady
A3. Gold In The Ground (3:10) Paul Grady
A4. Settin' The Woods On Fire (2:41) Ed G. Nelson, Fred Rose
A5. Good Old Country Baptizin' (2:39) Traditional

B1. Baby Boy (3:02) Mary Kay Place
B2. Get Acquainted Waltz (3:13) Charlie Louvin, Ira Louvin
B3. Coke And Chips (2:23) Paul Grady
B4. Just A Little Talk WIth Jesus (2:29) Robert Harkness
B5. All I Can Do (2:35) Dolly Parton

Not hearing it at first on "Heard It in a Love Song"

Carolina Dreams

Marshall Tucker Band

(1977)

Lead guitarist and primary songwriter Toy Caldwell had written a song that Doug Gray didn't like very much. Gray thought it was "too soft" for the Marshall Tucker Band.

For about a year, Gray drug his feet. He just didn't want to do the lead vocals on the song, and whenever there was an opportunity to go into the studio and record it, he kept putting it off.

"Finally, everybody looked at me and said, 'Go in there and cut the damn thing.' So I did. And once I cut it, what happened was quite remarkable," said Gray.

"Heard It in a Love Song" became the band's highest charting single in its history and would anchor Marshall Tucker's sixth studio album, *Carolina Dreams,* an ode to the band's hometown of Spartanburg, South Carolina.

"It was so extremely hard for me to look at the image of our band in the context of that song. The lyrics of it are 'I ain't never been with a woman long enough for my boots to get old.' I thought that might have been a bit insulting for a lot of people," said Gray. "Knowing that we was having fun out there with the women and whatever was going on. I thought it was too soft. Our image was being a bunch of redneck boys from South Carolina, and that song just didn't fit for me."

Doug Gray, lead singer for the Marshall Tucker Band, thought "Heard It in a Love Song" was "too soft" for the band. But it would go on to be a Top 20 hit. (Photo by Phil McAuliffe)

Gray said that Toy Caldwell agreed with him, that the song was too soft for the Marshall Tucker Band, even though Caldwell had written it and encouraged the band to record it with Gray on lead vocals.

"It finally came to me that we could have a ballad. To me, 'Heard It in a Love Song' is a ballad; it's just a faster ballad," said Gray. "When we put it out, we didn't have a clue how long it was going to take for it to be successful. You know, when you're a young band like that, you're just hoping to get somebody to pay attention to it. We'd walk in and I'd do that song and all these people would be screaming and yelling . . . like they do to this day. I'm still puzzled by it."

Up to this point, the Marshall Tucker Band had experienced quite a bit of success and was selling a lot of records. Its self-titled debut album had reached No. 29 on the U.S. Billboard 200 Albums chart in 1973 and featured the single "Can't You See." The band's fourth album, *Searchin' for a Rainbow,* had climbed even higher, making it to No. 15 on the albums chart, and featured its first Top 40 single,

"Fire on the Mountain," written by guitarist George McCorkle.

The Marshall Tucker Band had established itself in the Southern rock genre by 1976 when it went into the studio to record its fifth album, *Long Hard Ride.*

But after the album was released, sales for *Long Hard Ride* were disappointing.

"Everybody said, 'This doesn't make sense,' especially after selling a million records on the first album," said Gray. "Of course, we were out on the road for almost a year with the Allman Brothers and we were playing these songs that people were recognizing. And the songs were being played on the radio. But the sales were down. So nobody could figure out what was going on."

Eventually, the band just started working on its next album, *Carolina Dreams.*

"After *Long Hard Ride,* we said something is just not right. We really didn't spend a lot of time on *Carolina Dreams,* let's put it that way. But we put feeling into the songs," said Gray. "We put some of that worn-out feeling, that feeling that you get when you think, 'Oh, God, I could watch this movie and never have to get up and do a show or write a song.' So the pressure was kind of off. But at the same time, from the record label, the pressure was kind of on.

"Carolina Dreams was a record that was an ongoing mission. That's the beauty of that one. We would come home off the road and know that we had about four days, and we'd go down there and work on that record," said Gray.

Toy Caldwell wrote most of the songs for *Carolina Dreams,* although band members Gray, McCorkle, and Jerry Eubanks, who played the flute intro on "Heard It in a Love Song," also had writing credits on the album. Caldwell's brother, bassist Tommy Caldwell, and drummer Paul Riddle, didn't contribute any of the writing on the record.

Charlie Daniels had been playing and recording with the Marshall Tucker Band since 1973, so having him on the *Carolina Dreams* album wasn't unusual. (Photo by Phil McAuliffe)

Toy Caldwell's song "Desert Skies" on the album did feature the fiddle playing and harmony vocal of another Southern rock legend in the making at that time, Charlie Daniels.

Daniels first collaborated with the Marshall Tucker Band on its second album, *A New Life*, which was released in 1974 and certified as a gold album in 1977. And Daniels joined the band again for its third album, *Where We All Belong,* a double album that included one recorded in the studio and one recorded live. That album was released in 1974 and also certified gold.

"We decided we'd come out with *Where We All Belong* and that was the double album, partly recorded in Milwaukee at the Performing Arts Center [on July 31, 1974], which a lot of people weren't doing at the time," said Gray. "We were one of the few bands where our crowd would not tear up everything. They weren't rowdy. Hell, they're more rowdy now than they were then. We recorded two nights there plus we recorded a studio record. We just kind of freaked out a little bit because we didn't know what was going on. So we just decided to go into the studio when somebody had an idea, and we put it all together and made it work."

So by the time the band got to recording the *Carolina Dreams* album, having Charlie Daniels around to play on one of the tracks was commonplace.

"We had already been playing with Charlie in 1973. Him coming to Capricorn Records and being there and us being on tour together and running into each other in the middle of the night when the tour buses would pass was a lot of fun," said Gray. "Still to this day, when us and Charlie get together and do a show, we sit there and talk about the good old days, but we talk about the future as well. Ain't nobody getting no younger.

Carolina Dreams would make it to No. 23 on the U.S. Billboard 200 Albums chart, No. 22 on the Billboard Country chart, and No. 7 on the Canadian Albums chart. It is the band's only platinum album to date.

"Heard It in a Love Song" made it to No. 14 on the U.S. Billboard Hot 100 Singles chart, No. 51 on the Country chart, and No. 5 on the Canadian chart.

The Marshall Tucker Band would continue to experience success throughout the 1970s. Its *Together Forever* album, released in 1978, made it to No. 22 on the Billboard Albums chart, No. 26 on the Country chart, and No. 24 on the Canadian Albums chart; and its *Running Like the Wind* album, released in 1979, made it to No. 30 on the Billboard Albums chart. Neither of those albums produced a Top 40 single, though.

According to Gray, things changed for the Marshall Tucker Band in 1980 after the completion of the *Tenth* album. On April 22, 1980, the band's co-founder and bassist, Tommy Caldwell, was in a car accident and died six days later from massive head trauma.

The band tried to replace Tommy Caldwell with musicians who were friends, but it didn't work.

"Kind of the reason that it started changing was the result of the loneliness of not having somebody that's been there with you the whole time, basically that first seven years," said Gray. "It was kind of like you'd look over onstage and you might see Toy's best friend and one of our best friends, but it just didn't fill the gap. So the memories and the tales of the guys that have passed and all the women in our lives that have passed . . . it helps to gather strength when you have that many people to lean on."

The remaining original band members, with the exception of Gray and Eubanks, had split by 1983. What needed to be done in the 1980s after Tommy Caldwell's death according to Gray, was that somebody needed to take the band and lead it back to the powerful musical force that it had become in the 1970s.

"And everybody looked at me and said, hey man, you're the only one who can do it. You sing 99 percent of them songs, why not go out and take this on?" said Gray, who did just that and became the band's leader.

"When Toy and I shook hands and he wanted to leave — we all went to the same lawyer — so when he decided to leave, a couple of the other guys decided they wanted to leave as well, thinking that was a good thing to do. I kept thinking that the fans of the band have bought ten million to twenty million records from us, right? What would be the purpose of giving up on them when they've never given up on us? That was my way of thinking," said Gray.

Toy Caldwell died in 1993 and George McCorkle died in 2007. Drummer Paul Riddle still lives in Spartanburg and owns a drumstick company called Carolina Stick Company. Eubanks retired from performing in 1996. Gray is the lone remaining original member who has kept the Marshall Tucker Band legacy alive with different musicians, many of whom have been in the band for the past 25 years.

"When somebody about twenty-five or twenty-six years old comes up and they say, 'Man, my mom used to strap me into the car seat to come see you and now I'm bringing my daughter or my son to see you,' that's as much of a legacy as you can ask for," said Gray. "The beautiful part about all the stuff that we've done, it's always been fan-related or people-related. We're part of their family. We got our own families and grandkids and these people are bringing their families and grandkids and sending me pictures of their weddings and their dogs. Stuff like that."

Gray believes the Marshall Tucker Band has made a memorable contribution on the music scene, not just in the Southern rock genre of the 1970s, but for more than five decades.

"More or less, we had a partying reputation because Hank Junior would talk about coming to Spartanburg and partying with the Marshall Tucker Band, which we did. We pretty much had Skynyrd out there showing them the ropes, having fun the same way. But yet we were protective of our own selves. We watched over each other, never had any arguments," said Gray.

"People come up and say, man, y'all look like you had so much fun; I kept a permanent smile on my face as you played. That, I'm proud of," he said. "I think it's because of the memories created during that period of time. It's kind of unbelievable. It's all about the people and their moment in time with the Marshall Tucker Band."

Discography

Marshall Tucker Band

"Carolina Dreams"

Released January 1977

All songs written by Toy Caldwell except where noted.[3]

1. **Fly Like an Eagle (3:03)**
2. **Heard It in a Love Song (4:55)**
3. **I Should Have Never Started Lovin' You (7:10) Toy Caldwell, Doug Gray, George McCorkle**
4. **Life in a Song (3:33) Jerry Eubanks, McCorkle**
5. **Desert Skies (6:24)**
6. **Never Trust A Stranger (5:28)**
7. **Tell It To The Devil (6:45)**
8. **Silverado (bonus track, live, included on 2005 reissue. Recorded 1981 Winter Garden Theater, Dallas, TX) (4:28)**

A sensual song of physical and emotional longing

MAKE YOUR MOVE

Captain & Tennille

(1979)

The Captain and Tennille were living in Pacific Palisades, California, in what they called the house that "Love Will Keep Us Together" — their first No. 1 single — paid for. It was late 1978, they had just changed record labels, now signing with Casablanca Records, and they wanted their first album with the new company to be a good one.

Casablanca vice president Bruce Bird, and label head Neil Bogart, were sitting in the living room of the Pacific Palisades home one day with Captain Daryl Dragon and his wife, Toni Tennille, going over songs for an album.

Toward the end of the discussion, Tennille told the record executives she had one more song for them to consider.

"Let me play it for you and see what you think," Tennille recalls telling the executives. "So I sat at the piano and played it and Bruce jumped up and screamed 'That's a smash!' It shocked me. I said, 'Really?' And he said, 'Play it again.' And I did. They were hot for that song when I played it in my living room for them."

That's because it was indeed a hot song. "Do That to Me One More Time" would become the Captain & Tennille's second No. 1 single on the U.S. Billboard Hot 100 Singles chart and anchor the duo's first album for Casablanca, *Make Your Move,* released in 1979.

Captain & Tennille had entered the music scene four years earlier, in 1975, when their debut album *Love Will Keep Us Together* was released by A&M Records. The album would peak at No. 2 on the Billboard 200 Albums chart. The title track, written by Neil Sedaka and Howard Greenfield and featured on Sedaka's 1974 album *Sedaka's Back,* was a No. 1 hit for Captain & Tennille on both the Billboard Hot 100 Singles chart and the Billboard Easy Listening chart. The song would also be the best-selling single of 1975 and would win the Grammy Award for Record of the Year in 1976.

Over the next few years, Captain & Tennille would release a string of hit singles for A&M Records, including "The Way I Want to Touch You," "Lonely Night (Angel Face)," "Shop Around," and "Muskrat Love."

The duo had developed a "wholesome" reputation with its music and public persona, and had become so popular by the mid-1970s that Captain & Tennille had their own television variety show, which ran on ABC from September 1976 to March 1977.

They had recorded three Billboard Top 20 albums, all of which went gold or platinum. In 1978, Captain & Tennille recorded what would be their last album for A&M Records, titled *Dream,* which included the single "You've Never Done It Like That," another Sedaka/Greenfield song that reached No. 10 on the U.S. Billboard Hot 100 Singles chart.

But the music industry was changing at that point in the 1970s, and A&M Records was trying to change with it. The record company's focus had shifted away from soft rock.

In early 1978, A&M Records decided to release a Captain & Tennille *Greatest Hits* album. Although that record didn't break into the Top 50 on the charts, it, too, became a gold album.

But that didn't sit well with Captain & Tennille. They thought the record company's decision to release a *Greatest Hits* album meant that A&M didn't think the duo could produce any more hits.

It was around that time that Casablanca Records had let Captain & Tennille know that it was interested in signing the duo for the label. And the disappointment that both Tennille and Dragon had with A&M over the *Greatest Hits* release made the timing right in their minds to make the switch to Casablanca, according to Tennille.

Casablanca, though, wasn't known at the time for promoting a "wholesome" style of music, with groups like KISS and Village People among its stable of artists.

Which was good, because that wholesome reputation that Captain & Tennille had developed didn't even square with Tennille herself.

"That's what everybody read into the girl-next-door thing. But I've always been a very sexual and sensual woman. And I wrote the way I felt about Daryl, even though it wasn't reciprocated," said Tennille.

"It always used to make me laugh because I remember when we recorded 'The Way I Want to Touch You,' we were promoting it with A&M after it was released as our second single," said Tennille. "I think we were in Saint Louis and the top adult contemporary station at the time refused to play it because they thought it was too explicit. I just had to laugh, because I thought, well, wait a minute, it's not explicit, it's what's in your mind. Some people get it and some people don't because they don't look for it. Just because you appear to be [the] girl next door – and I'm a nice person, I can't help it, that's the way I was raised – but that doesn't mean that I'm not a sensual person."

"Do That to Me One More Time" marked a bit of a comeback for Captain & Tennille and propelled the *Make Your Move* album to No. 23 on the U.S. Billboard 200

Albums chart.

But the song, like many of the other suggestive songs that Tennille sang — primarily to Dragon — was lost on the Captain. That's because the marriage itself was a one-sided affair, with Tennille expressing her love over and over, without her husband responding.

It was something that the public never knew about at the time.

"Daryl didn't look at the lyrics at all. I didn't really realize that because every time that we were in concert or something like that and I would sing these songs, I would be singing them to him," said Tennille. "Those were my feelings. But having lived with him for so many years, I knew what he was thinking. He wasn't listening to me saying the way I want to touch you or any of that stuff. He was probably going, 'Oh, my God, the bass doesn't sound right. Let's get the mix better.' That was where his brain was, not in the words that I was singing."

Dragon would write instrumentals for the duo, but he didn't write songs that people could sing because, according to Tennille, "he didn't do lyrics."

"I don't think he cared about lyrics or how much they mean to a lot of people. When they hear a song and hear words, they can substitute in their own minds when they are listening. He never did anything like that," said Tennille.

In her book, *Toni Tennille: A Memoir,* she describes "Do That to Me One More Time" as "a sensual song of physical and emotional longing, which of course reflected my feelings for my distant husband."

The fact that it became Captain & Tennille's second No. 1 single also had significant meaning for Tennille. "And even sweeter was the knowledge that this song had been written by me, not someone else as many of our other hits had been," wrote Tennille in her book. "Its tremendous success cemented the confidence that I really was a songwriter and that I could write songs with hit potential."

The cover photo for *Make Your Move* shows Tennille looking lovingly into the eyes of Dragon, who appears, it could be subjectively argued now, to not be returning that loving feeling.

"That Captain & Tennille image — throughout the '70s and into the '80s and on — wasn't reciprocated," said Tennille. "I still was hopeful that I would eventually break through to him."

Captain & Tennille would record only one more album for Casablanca, *Keeping Our Love Warm,* released in 1980. That album, too, portrayed the couple as sensual and loving as evidenced by the album cover, which featured a barely clothed Captain and Tennille in a bathhouse. The album featured songs like "Keeping Our Love Warm" and "Gentle Stranger," both written by Tennille and suggesting a longing for the Captain to return the love and affection that Tennille had for him.

"To me, his life is a very tiny life. He lives it inside himself. He is not open. I just think of all the joyful experiences that I've had with music and family and friends. All that stuff. And he had closed himself off from that pretty much ever since I've known him," said Tennille. "I still thought — and I kept hoping — I know people thought what we had was perfect. I thought, it isn't, but it's going to be. I'm going to get there."

Eventually, Tennille gave up on the relationship. It would take years for her to realize that she finally needed to make a change in her life.

"But then I began to realize, about the time we moved to Prescott, Arizona around 2007, that Daryl's extreme negativity and his constant the-world-is-going-to-hell-in-a-hand-basket approach was dragging me down into the same hole with him," she said. "My natural positivity and good outlook on life was starting to be just drained from me. And it really scared me. And I thought, you know what, I'm going to have to separate myself from this man so I can go ahead and live my life."

Still, it took her several more years to make a final break with Dragon. She was 73 years old when she finally divorced him in 2013.

"I realized I had to do what I had to do. I still care about Daryl. He is the only man that I ever loved. Period," said Tennille. "Of course, during the time we were together, I had lots of various and sundry men approach me. None of them could stand up in my mind to what Daryl could have been, not what he was. So I just said I'm keeping my vows because that's what I said I was going to do. And I thought I was going to do that for the rest of my life . . . until I couldn't stand it any longer."

The release of her 2016 autobiography, co-written by her niece, Caroline Tennille St. Clair, laid bare all those emotions and experiences and revealed that eventually love wouldn't keep Captain & Tennille together.

"I called him and said, 'You know, Daryl, I'm going to write the memoir; Caroline and I are working on it.' And I said you understand that this is my point of view. I'm writing it from the way I saw our relationship and my life," said Tennille. "And he said, and this is an absolute quote: 'I'm not worried. You've always been a straight shooter.' He knew that I would not vilify him because he doesn't deserve it. He is who he is because of his own circumstances.

"None of this is his fault. And none of it is anybody's fault. I have no regrets. He made me the most creative I've ever been in my life when I started working with him. He really thought I was a great singer and songwriter. Whenever I would play him a new song, he would go right into the studio and make a record of it. That encouraged his creativity, too. So we did that for each other."

As for the popularity of Captain & Tennille in the

1970s, Tennille said she's not sure why they rocketed to the top of the music industry during that era.

"We just did what we do. It just happened that way. I've always just gone ahead and been what I am. And Daryl was the same way. He was the man you saw on the TV show. That was him. He didn't make up a character," said Tennille. "Somehow with my ability to kind of translate him to the audience, he created this character that people were just intrigued with. They were fascinated with that guy. But boy, that was him. There was nothing about that that was made up."

And as of 2016, Tennille was still unsure, at age 76, if her book project would encourage her to go back to performing.

"There is one thing that has always frightened me throughout my whole career. I used ask people I trusted, like Daryl and other people, to tell me when they thought I wasn't singing up to my best," said Tennille. "That's not to say I'm not. But I'm afraid to go out and try again. I've been dormant for so long.

"The thing that I tend to want to do now is to be under the radar. I did that for so long, keeping my head down and not doing any interviews. I've never talked about my fears of singing again to anyone," she said. "I've taken some time to try to figure it out. Staying under the radar, that's what I want to do. I'd love to do more narrating for other authors. I'd love to do voice work for animated features and things like that."

But Tennille hasn't completely dismissed the possibility of singing again.

"Maybe somebody will convince me to come out and sing a couple of tunes someday," she said. "It's wonderful to know — and I'm realizing more even now — what our music meant to people and the memories that they had. That was a lot of fun."

Discography

The Captain and Tennille
"Make Your Move"
Released 1979

1. **Love on a Shoestring (3:37) Kerry Chater, Douglas L.A. Foxworthy**
2. **No Love in the Morning (4:05) Robert Bellarmine Byrne-**
3. **Deep in the Dark (5:28) Toni Tennille**
4. **How Can You Be So Cold (7:04) Toni Tennille**
5. **Do That to Me One More Time (4:17) Toni Tennille**
6. **Happy Together (A Fantasy) (5:26) Alan Gordon, Garry Bonner**
7. **Baby You Still Got It (5:32) Toni Tennille**
8. **Never Make Your Move Too Soon (5:57) Nesbert Hooper Jr., Will Jennings**

A well-established goody two-shoes goes sexy

SELF-TITLED

Karen Carpenter

(1980 and 1996)

Karen Carpenter was a perfectionist. But she was having trouble during a recording session in late 1979 with the phrasing of the song "Still in Love with You," which she planned to include on her self-titled solo album *Karen Carpenter.*

The Carpenters had enjoyed a decade of huge success in the 1970s with a dozen Top 10 singles, four Top 10 albums, 18 Grammy nominations, and three Grammys.

Now, at age 29, Karen Carpenter was making an album for the first time without her brother, Richard Carpenter, who was battling an addiction to Quaaludes.

Karen didn't want to sit idle musically while Richard was recovering. She also wanted to do something that was quite un-Carpenter-like: to make an album that would shed the duo's well-established goody two-shoes image that had been carefully crafted up to that point.

Karen Carpenter wanted to take a sexier approach with her music. And producer Phil Ramone encouraged her.

According to a *New York Times* article by Rob Hoerburger on October 6, 1996, Ramone had been a fan of Karen's voice, but didn't want to make sexually clueless songs like "Sing," a No. 3 single for the Carpenters, and "Top of the World," their second No. 1 hit.

Liberty DeVitto, a member of Billy Joel's band The Lords of 52nd Street, had just finished recording Joel's *Glass Houses* album when he signed on to play on Karen Carpenter's solo album.
(Photo by Mike Morsch)

"I said to her, 'A lot of your fans aren't teenagers anymore. Why don't you grow up with them?'" Hoerburger quoted Ramone as saying in his *New York Times* article.

Ramone had just finished producing Billy Joel's album *Glass Houses,* which would be released in March 1980, go to No. 1 on the U.S. Billboard 200 Albums chart, and win a Grammy in 1981 for Best Rock Vocal Performance — Male.

Joel's band, which Ramone had named the Lords of 52nd Street after Joel's 1978 album *52nd Street,* was available and Ramone believed the band members would be perfect co-conspirators to help Karen transform her girl-next-door image for her next album.

Among the Lords of 52nd Street whom Ramone enlisted to work with Karen were bassist Doug Stegmeyer, drummer Liberty DeVitto, and guitarist Russell Javors.

Karen had listened to about 200 songs in an effort to come up with the 12 that she wanted to use on the album. Among those that she really liked was "Still in Love With You," which was written by Javors.

Russell Javors, guitarist for The Lords of 52nd Street, wrote two songs and played on Karen Carpenter's solo album (Photo by Mike Morsch)

"I couldn't understand what Karen would see in my songs because they were very different than anything that she did," said Javors. "And we were going to be the band on the majority of the tracks through Phil. So either way, I would have gotten to work with Karen. And it was so amazing."

But Karen was struggling with getting the vocals the way she wanted them on "Still in Love with You."

"She was having a little trouble with the vocal because it was a real rocker. That wasn't what Karen was, and she was trying to fit her voice into the track," said Javors. "And she literally had me in the booth with her while she was doing the vocal. We were nose to nose and I was lip-syncing and she was trying to copy the phrasing. I was really impressed that she liked it enough that she would have me do that and that she was such a perfectionist and was really going for it."

Another Javors song, "All Because of You," made it onto the album as well. A third Javors-penned song was recorded, but did not make it onto the album.

In addition to the Lords of 52nd Street, Ramone had brought in Rob Mounsey, a young session musician with whom he had worked on several other projects. Mounsey had not been much of a songwriter up to that point in his career, but he did have a song called "Guess I Just Lost My Head" that Ramone liked.

"Phil asked me to sing it for Karen and she liked it," said Mounsey. "But she had to change a line. Right at the beginning of the song, it says 'I really don't mean to stare, I was only watching the flower in your hair.' When it becomes a woman's song though, she can't be looking at a guy with a flower in his hair. That's weird. She had to change 'the flower in your hair' line. Which was one of my favorite lines when I did it. I couldn't really think of anything because I'm always not that great with lyrics. But she came up with 'I was only trying to memorize you there.' I thought that actually was pretty good. It's pretty clever because it connects with the whole story and feeling of the lyric."

In addition to those songs, Karen chose to cover Paul Simon's "Still Crazy After All These Years"; and then stuck to the sexier theme with "Making Love in the Afternoon," written by Peter Cetera, who also provided vocals on the song; "Remember When Lovin' Took All Night" by John Farrar and Molly-Ann Leiken; "My Body Keeps Changing My Mind" by Leslie Pearl; and two songs by Rod Temperton, including "Lovelines" and "If We Try." Karen filled out the album with "If I Had You" by Steve Dorff, Gary Harju, and Larry Herbstritt; and "Last One Singin' the Blues" by Pete McCann.

"Musically, it really was a departure from the Carpenters' earlier stuff. She always used to sing in this really low, buttery alto that everybody loved. She didn't do that so much on this record," said Mounsey. "It was the late 1970s and the songs were different. A lot of the songs tended to be sexually explicit, which was a little strange for Karen and her personality. She was maybe a little bit square. She was the good girl from Downing, California."

Despite the calculated effort to make the *Karen Carpenter* album more adult-oriented, Karen was still Karen. According to Mounsey, the no-holds-barred salty language frequently used by the Lords of 52nd Street band members during the recording sessions didn't go unnoticed by Karen.

"She sort of got a little bit upset when the musicians would curse. The f-word upset her and she would sort of blanche a little bit at that," said Mounsey.

But for the most part, Karen took it all in stride. In an interview with Jeb Wright for *Classic Rock Revisited*, drummer DeVitto, with whom Karen had formed a bond because she also was a drummer, relates a story about how the Lords of 52nd Street behaved around Karen.

"When I was recording the *Glass Houses* album, we were also recording for Karen. It was my birthday and Phil Ramone ordered me a cake from the Erotic Baker. It had a penis on it. It was funny to be with Karen and getting a penis cake delivered. I have a picture of me holding her hand above the cake and pushing it down. She is like, 'I've never been this close to one of these before!' She was great," said DeVitto in the *Classic Rock Revisited* interview.

"I don't remember anything about her not liking the swearing, but we didn't hold back in front of her. It was just playful," said Javors. "Phil told us to treat her like one of the guys. We were kind of rowdy in the studio. We always had a lot of respect and were professional, but we always had fun. We were a little over the top sometimes."

Neither Javors nor Mounsey recall Karen having any health issues, particularly with anorexia nervosa, during the recording of the album.

"I would have never have guessed that. I don't exactly have anorexia radar, so I would never have known. But she seemed to be in good health and she seemed happy. I think she was. I think she really enjoyed doing the record and that she really liked it," said Mounsey.

But there were other issues ahead once the *Karen Carpenter* album was finished. According to the 1995 book *The Carpenters: The Untold Story* by Ray Coleman, although executives at A&M Records — the Carpenters' label — had approved the material, they didn't much like the finished album. Herb Alpert and Jerry Moss — the A&M of A&M Records — urged Karen not to release the album. There were reports at the time that even Richard Carpenter didn't like the album and didn't want it released.

"I don't know the real story on that. I was at the playback session though," said Javors. "There was a bunch of the bigwigs there and it was really uncomfortable."

Ramone confirmed that scenario in the 1996 *New York Times* article. Alpert, Moss, and Richard Carpenter were all at that initial playback session of the album.

"She was expecting them to come up and hug her after every track," Ramone is quoted as saying in the article. "But they just sat there."

In that same article, Alpert said he liked, but didn't love, the album. "It just didn't ring my bell the way a Carpenters album would," he said in the article.

Alpert added in that article that Karen vacillated between loving the album and hating it, but the Ramone camp didn't buy that, according to the article. "This wasn't a woman given to tears," Ramone is quoted as saying. "When she was upset, she just wouldn't eat. But when we got out of that meeting and far enough away, she just crumpled in my arms."

According to Richard Carpenter, Karen eventually decided to respect the opinions of the record company officials and it was her decision to shelve the record in 1980.

Her battle with anorexia continued to consume her, though, and she died on February 4, 1983.

"What an unbelievable loss. She had such a beautiful voice and was really a beautiful person," said Javors.

"Karen was very nice to me," said Mounsey. "One time she was talking to Phil and they were talking about me. And Karen said, 'He's kind of like a young Richard.' I thought that was a really nice compliment because she loved her brother and she had a lot of respect for his abilities. She was really a great person. It was crushing when she died."

According to the *New York Times* article, Karen had called Ramone on February 2, 1983, just 36 hours before she died, and the conversation eventually got around to her solo album.

In the article, Ramone said the conversation went like this:

Karen: "Can I use the f-word?"

Ramone: "You're a grown woman. Say whatever you want."

Karen: "It's a fucking great album."

The *Karen Carpenter* album was eventually released in 1996, 13 years after her death. Both Richard Carpenter and Phil Ramone offered statements about the album.

Richard wrote: "For personal reasons, which have been chronicled in other sources, I needed and decided to take a leave of absence from our career in 1979. Karen, who was not interested in remaining idle during my hiatus, elected to record a solo album. To produce the album, Herb Alpert suggested Phil Ramone, a highly talented and successful producer who had enjoyed both critical and commercial success with such artists as Paul Simon and Billy Joel.

"Phil signed on, and on April 30, 1979, Karen left LA for New York, with the first session commencing on May 2. Due to some scheduling conflicts, the album was not delivered until early 1980.

"Upon completion of the playback, the reaction of A&M executives and others, including myself, was lukewarm.

"As time passes and events unfold, one's perspective on certain matters can change, as has mine regarding this album.

Karen was with us precious little time. She was a great artist. This album represents a certain period and change of approach in her career. As such it deserves to be heard in its entirety as originally delivered . . . plus one bonus track." — Richard Carpenter.

Ramone stated: "To completely understand the love and adventure of Karen's solo project, people should know that we made a conscious decision to experiment with music and styles that were not in the Carpenters' albums. We wanted their fans, as well as a new audience, to hear one of the greatest voices in a different surrounding. We knew some things were trendy and that the intimate songs would express her love of all music.

"It was inconceivable to those of us involved with the project that a rumor might spread regarding the end of the Carpenters. That truly was beyond the realm of possibility: Karen loved Richard and the music they made together. I've always related to Richard's arrangements and composing with deep admiration and we remain friends.

"The love of Billy Joel's band — Rod Temperton and the other players, who had the best time working with her — gave Karen Carpenter's work in New York a sparkle that can be heard on this album. Karen and the rest of us who worked on this project understood the decision to wait on the release.

"As years passed, both Richard and I wondered when it might be released. Together we stand proud as this was a piece of work that meant so much to Karen; it truly was a labor of love.

"I have not remixed or done anything to the tapes. These mixes, the material and style, are the way Karen approved them. The bonus track is unmixed and was one of several that might have been finished.

"I miss her terribly, but I know she's watching with a smile.

"And to Richard: Thank you for letting me borrow your sister for this album." — Phil Ramone.

For one of the musicians who played on the album, though, by the time it was released, the world had continued to evolve musically.

"I thought it was really a great record, and even though I enjoyed it, it struck me as kind of stylistically dated by the time it was released," said Mounsey. "It was a period of tremendous change [from 1980 to its release in 1996] in music technology and the way that affected music styles. All kinds of stuff had happened in the meantime. So it did strike me as a relic of the late 1970s, although I think it's a really good record and there is a lot of great stuff on it."

Discography

Karen Carpenter
Self-titled

Recorded May 1979 through January 1980
Released Oct. 8, 1996

1. Lovelines (5:06) Rod Temperton)
2. All Because of You (3:31) Russell Javors)
3. If I Had You (3:54) Steve Dorff, Gary Harju, Larry Herbstritt)
4. Making Love in the Afternoon (featuring Peter Cetera) (3:57) Peter Cetera)
5. If We Try (3:46) Rod Temperton)
6. Remember When Lovin' Took All Night (3:50) John Farrar, Molly-Ann Leiken)
7. Still in Love with You (3:15) Russell Javors)
8. "My Body Keeps Changing My Mind" (3:46) Leslie Pearl)
9. Make Believe It's Your First Time (3:12) Bob Morrison, Johnny Wilson)
10. Guess I Just Lost My Head (3:36) Rob Mounsey)
11. Still Crazy After All These Years (4:17) Paul Simon)
12. Last One Singin' the Blues (bonus track) (3:29) Pete McCann)

Acknowledgements

As has been the case with each volume of this series, a group of highly skilled professionals has collaborated to produce *The Vinyl Dialogues Volume IV: From Studio to Stylus.*

My mentor and friend Frank D. Quattrone has served as the first editor for all the books in the series, and he once again has lent his considerable editing skills to this effort. Joining him this time is another mentor and friend, Aubrey Huston, a longtime editor and former boss. Between the two of them, the copy was pretty clean by the time it got to the final edit, once again by Ruth Littner and Ann Stolinsky of Gemini Wordsmiths (www.geminiwordsmiths.com), who fact-checked and fine-tuned the content. I am fortunate to have the skilled and professional help of all four of these fine editors.

The cover was designed by Mat Shetler and David Munoz-Mendoza. Mat, who happens to be my son-in-law, and David, are art students at Penn State-Abington in Pennsylvania. They put a lot of time, thought, and effort into the design of the front and back covers of this book, and they did a tremendous job.

Once again, photographer Phil McAuliffe has provided wonderful images of some of the artists interviewed and mentioned in these pages. Phil, a former colleague in the newspaper business, is also a singer-songwriter. He knows a lot about music and about taking photographs of musicians.

The artists interviewed for this volume were gracious with their time and storytelling. I dealt directly with many of them, including Bob Berryhill of The Surfaris; Jim Yester of The Association; Stephen Bishop; Jon Carroll of the Starland Vocal Band; Rob Mouncey; Elliot Lurie of Looking Glass; and Mary Kay Place, who agreed to be interviewed on a recommendation of my dear friends, Gail Farrell and Ron Anderson, stars of the *Lawrence Welk Show*.

For the artists who I could not reach directly, I had the help of some very professional publicists and agents in the music industry, including: Paki Newell of CO5 Media in Los Angeles, who represents Brian Wilson and Blondie Chaplin of the Beach Boys; Steve Rosenbaum, representing Marilyn McCoo and Billy Davis, Jr.; Jim Anderson, who put me in touch with Dennis Tufano of The Buckinghams, Frank Jeckell of the 1910 Fruitgum Company, Shirley Alston Reeves of the Shirelles, Peter Noone of Herman's Hermits, and Gary Puckett; Hana Ali, representing Timothy B. Schmit; Jeff Albright of Albright Entertainment Group, who represents Jimmy Ryan and Lee Shapiro; Andy Gilmartin, who represents the Lords of 52nd Street, including Liberty DeVitto and Russell Javors; Emily Anderson, assistant to Paul Anka; Dan Bauer, who helped set up an interview with Russell Thompkins, Jr. of the Stylistics; Harlan Boll, publicist for Toni Tennille; Kay Waggoner of Absolute Publicity, representing Danny Hutton of Three Dog Night; Melissa Kucirek, representing Felix Cavaliere of the Rascals; Stephanie Elliott, assistant to Ken Kaplan of the Gersh Agency, who arranged the interview with Mary Kay Place; and Randy Alexander of Randex Communications, who always helps me when I ask.

Special thanks to colleague Anthony Stoeckert, entertainment editor at Packet Media in Princeton, New Jersey, who approves my story ideas and allows me to write about music for his section; and to my publisher Bob Sims of Biblio Publishing out of Columbus, Ohio, who has published all five of my books, including all the volumes of *The Vinyl Dialogues*.

And as always, I couldn't have taken on this project without the support of my family: wife, Judy Wiesenhutter Morsch; daughter Kiley and husband, Mat Shetler; daughter Lexi; stepdaughter, Kaitie Hughes; and stepson, Kevin Hughes.

Sources

Author interview with Shirley Alston Reeves of the Shirelles on October 17, 2016.

Author interview with Bob Berryhill of The Surfaris on September 1, 2016; additional statements are from the book, *Wipe Out: The Story of the Surfaris*, by Bob Berryhill, original guitarist and founding member. Published by Salttalk Productions, 2016.

Author interview with Peter Noone of Herman's Hermits on September 17, 2015.

Author interview with Carl Giammerese of The Buckinghams on September 24, 2015; author interview with Dennis Tufano of The Buckinghams on March 27, 2017.

Author interview with Peter Yarrow on October 7, 2015; author interview with Paul Prestopino on November 3, 2015.

Author interview with Felix Cavaliere of the Young Rascals on May 10, 2016; author interview with Dino Danelli, April 2013.

Author interview with Jim Yester of The Association on September 12, 2016; author interviews with Michael Brewer and Tom Shipley on November 2, 2016.

Author interview with Gary Puckett of Gary Puckett and the Union Gap on September 16, 2015.

Author interview with Frank Jeckell of the 1910 Fruitgum Company on March 10, 2017.

Author interview with Marilyn McCoo and Billy Davis, Jr. of the 5th Dimension on May 24, 2016.

Author interview with Danny Hutton of Three Dog Night on September 13, 2016.

Author interview with Timothy B. Schmit on April 11, 2017; Eddie Winters interview with Richie Furay, October 7, 2015; Daniel Coston of *The Coston Chronicles* interview with Richie Furay on June 26, 2012; Ken Sharp of *Rockcellar* magazine interview with Randy Meisner on November 10, 2016; John Beaudin of *Rock History* interview with Randy Meisner on August 4, 2000.

Author interview with Russell Thompkins, Jr. of the Stylistics on November 11, 2016; National Public Radio "Fresh Air" interview by Terry Gross with Thom Bell; *Billboard* magazine story and interview with Thom Bell on June 16, 2006.

Author interview with Jimmy Ryan on February 20, 2017; *Boys in the Trees: A Memoir* by Carly Simon, copyright 2015 by Flatiron Books.

Author interview with Blondie Chaplin on August 4, 2016; *I Am Brian Wilson* by Brian Wilson with Ben Greenmail, copyright 2016, published by Da Capo Press; *Good Vibrations: My Life as a Beach Boy* by Mike Love with James S. Hirsch, copyright 2016 by Blue Rider Press; *Rolling Stone* review by Stephen Davis, first published June 22, 1972; *Rolling Stone* review by Jim Miller, first published March 1, 1973.

Author interview with Elliot Lurie of Looking Glass on January 19, 2017.

Author interview with Danny O'Keefe on July 18, 2016.

Author interview with Paul Anka on November 18, 2016; *My Way: An Autobiography*, by Paul Anka, with David Dalton, published in 2013 by St. Martin's Press.

Author interview with Lee Shapiro of the Four Seasons on January 17, 2017.

Author interview with Ron Dante on May 23, 2017; author interview with Bruce Johnston on July 23, 2013; *Clive Davis: The Soundtrack of My Life* by Clive Davis with Anthony DeCurtis, copyright 2013 by Simon & Schuster.

Author interview with Jon Carroll of the Starland Vocal Band on October 12, 2016; Bill Danoff website, www.billdanoff.com.

Author interview with Stephen Bishop on October 7, 2016.

Author interview with Jeffrey Leynor of the Stanky Brown Group on July 1, 2016; *New York Times* review by Robert Palmer, published June 27, 1978.

Author interview with Mary Kay Place on April 18, 2017.

Author interview with Doug Gray of the Marshall Tucker Band on September 26, 2016.

Author interview with Toni Tennille on June 3, 2016; *Toni Tennille: A Memoir* by Toni Tennille and Caroline Tennille St. Clair, Taylor Trade Publishing, copyright 2016.

Author interview with Russell Javors of the Lords of 52nd Street on December 6, 2016; author interview with Rob Mouncey on November 29, 2016; *New York Times* article by Rob Hoerburger from October 6, 1996; *Classic Rock Revisited* interview by Jeb Wright with Liberty DeVitto.

About the Author

Mike Morsch has been a reporter, editor, and columnist for more than 40 years at newspapers in Iowa, Illinois, Pennsylvania, and New Jersey.

He has earned numerous awards for his writing from the Illinois Press Association, the Pennsylvania Newspapers Association, the Philadelphia Press Association, the Local Media Association, and the New Jersey Press Association.

This is his fifth book for Biblio Publishing, which includes all four volumes of *The Vinyl Dialogues*. The first three volumes of the series have been accepted by the Rock and Roll Hall of Fame for inclusion in its archives and library.

The Vinyl Dialogues website, www.vinyldialogues.com, includes Mike's blog, which features regular columns and photographs about music from the 1960s and 1970s. There is also a *Vinyl Dialogues* Facebook page and Twitter account.

A 1982 graduate of the University of Iowa, Mike earned a Bachelor of Science degree in journalism and was a two-year letterman on the Hawkeyes' baseball team.

He is currently an editor for Packet Media in Princeton, New Jersey. You can reach him by email at msquared35@yahoo.com.

Index